A TEEN'S GUIDE

TO

LIFE SKILLS

a teen's guide to money management, people skills, cooking, cleaning and all the adulting stuff you need to know.

TEEN THRIVE

MEDICAL DISCLAIMER

This book does not contain medical [medical referring to mental and physical health throughout his disclaimer] and health advice. The health information contained in this book is provided for general information and educational purposes only and is not intended as and shall not be understood or construed as professional medical advice, diagnosis or treatment, or substitute for professional medical advice, diagnosis, or treatment. Before taking any action based upon such information, we expressly recommend that you seek advice from medical professionals. Your use of the book, including the implementation of any suggestions or recommendations laid out in the book, does not create a doctor-patient relationship. Your use of the book is solely at your own risk, and you expressly agree not to rely upon any information contained in the book as a substitute for professional medical advice, diagnosis, or treatment. Under no circumstances shall Teen Thrive be held liable or responsible for any errors or omissions in the book or for any damage you may suffer with respect to any actions taken or not taken based on any or all of the contents of the book. and/ or as a result of failing to seek competent advice from medical professionals.

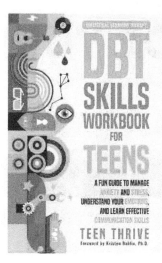

CHECK OUT OUR OTHER BOOKS

WE'VE GOT A BONUS FOR YOU!

FREE

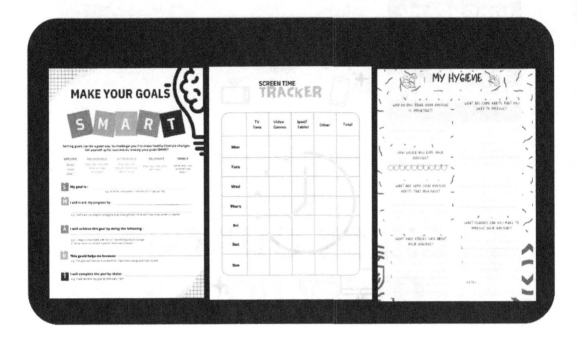

A SET OF 10 LIFESKILLS WORKSHEETS

TAKE EVERYTHING YOU LEARNED EVEN FURTHER, WITH THIS UNIQUE SET OF 10 WORKSHEETS THAT HAVE BEEN CREATIVELY DESIGNED FOR YOU TO HAVE FUN AND GET ORGANIZED.

ALL YOU HAVE TO DO IS PRINT THEM OUT AND GET STARTED!

SCAN ME

OR VISIT:
https://bonus.teen-thrive.com/lifeskills-worksheets

TABLE OF CONTENTS

INTRODUCTION

The day before my high school graduation, I found myself standing in front of my bedroom mirror, sobbing hysterically. I didn't know what to wear for the ceremony. I didn't know what I was going to say in my speech as the class president. I was nervous about packing for college, about how much (not very much!) money I had saved up for my freshman year, and I was terrified to leave my small town for big city college life. At the time, these challenges seemed insurmountable. I felt young, dumb, and broke but,

> **I was better equipped than I thought to enter the "real world," as they call it.**

You might assume I was automatically more resilient because I came from a wealthy family, or perhaps one that had taken the time to personally teach me everything I needed to know to be successful in college.

As a first generation college student, I did not come from money, and I did not come from a family that knew a lot about college life. However, I did come from a family that valued the importance of life skills.

I was fortunate enough to have parents who let me figure things out on my own while also giving me the tools I needed to find these important answers to these important questions for myself. Surprisingly, I would later learn that I was in the minority. During the pandemic, about 30% of recent college graduates moved back in with their parents, and 81% of respondents to an Experian boost survey said they wished they were taught more life skills before graduating college.

I was nervous before going to college, but after college, I was in a great place. I knew how to manage myself, my money, and my personal business and I never had to move back in with my parents, even when times were more challenging:

WHAT EXACTLY ARE LIFE SKILLS?

If you've picked up this book, chances are, you might already have a bit of an inkling.
Life skills are the crucial strategies, skills, and understandings you need to be successful out in the real world.

Life skills might include everything from financial literacy to good time management to even a basic understanding of how to groom and care for one's personal hygiene. They don't necessarily have anything to do with getting a college degree. They're simply the skills you need to be a successful adult.

That's not to say that I have everything all figured out. Although my parents did a good job of teaching me how to be a functional adult, at times, I find myself, now in my mid thirties, staring blankly back at that mirror again filled with anxiety about what my next steps should be.

SO HOW DO YOU GET THOSE TOOLS?

You've already made a great first step in filling up your toolbox. If you're a teen who's wondering how to be a successful adult and perhaps you're not sure where to start this book is for you. I'll guide you through everything you need to know to become a confident, happy, and secure young adult.

Whether you're headed off to college or you still have a few years left of high school, it's never too late to start learning how to take care of yourself, your home, and your business.

LET'S GET STARTED!

PART 1
Taking Care of Yourself

We live in a society where we are taught to look out for numero uno. That can be construed both negatively and positively. On one hand, it might seem a bit selfish to focus wholly on yourself. To be fair, it's important to consider the role you play in others' lives and vice versa. However, you can't take care of others until you have a good grasp on who you are as a person That starts with taking care of yourself. And that's the first crucial life skill we'll cover in this book.

To be a successful adult, you need to know how to manage your own physical, mental, and emotional well being. You can't tend to the other areas of your life (like your finances and your home) until you are healthy and able to present yourself in a positive light.

SO HOW DO YOU DO THAT? LET'S TAKE A CLOSER LOOK.

Chapter 1: Hygiene & Physical Care

If you want to be successful, you need to look the part. Our first set of life skills has to do with taking care of your own mental health and physical hygiene, as well as how you appear to others.

They say not to judge a book by its cover, but the reality is that we do. While everybody has an off day here and there, it's important to remember that first impressions matter. By presenting yourself as someone who cares about his or her own appearance, you'll find that tasks and interactions come much easier in life. To get started, I want you to write down a few notes.

HOW DO YOU THINK YOU PRESENT YOURSELF TO OTHERS?

_____

_____

_____

_____

_____

AND HOW WOULD YOU LIKE TO PRESENT YOURSELF IN A PERFECT WORLD?

_____

_____

_____

_____

Not-so-Appropriate Self-Presentation

Appropriate Self-Presentation

FIRST JOB INTERVIEW

Not-so-Appropriate Self-Presentation

Appropriate Self-Presentation

BODY LANGUAGE

WHAT'S YOUR CURRENT HYGIENE ROUTINE LIKE?

Be honest and rate your current hygiene routine

How often do you:
take care of your nails properly?

wash your face?

Wipe away your makeup?

Shave your legs?

Inspect your piercings?

How often do you:
Shave and wash your face?

Clip your toenails?

Put on deodorant?

Clean your feet?

Brush your hair?

PHYSICAL HYGIENE

As teens, we are often preoccupied with our appearance, especially as we start to socialize and become more active in our communities. But good personal hygiene goes beyond having a clean and neat outward appearance: it's about taking the necessary steps to ensure that we stay healthy and well.

Taking care of yourself doesn't have to be a chore; it's simply a part of self-care that should be practiced daily!

WHY GOOD PERSONAL HYGIENE MATTERS

Good personal hygiene is more than just a habit, it's an important part of our overall health and well being. Everything from preventing the spread of germs to looking and feeling good starts with proper hygiene.

The most obvious benefit of good personal hygiene is that it helps prevent illness by stopping the spread of bacteria and viruses. Washing your hands regularly, especially before eating or after using the restroom, can reduce your risk of becoming sick from bacteria or viruses. Taking regular showers or baths also helps keep your body free from dirt, sweat, and other potential sources of infection.

Good personal hygiene can also help maintain self confidence. Everyone likes to look their best when they go out in public but feeling clean and fresh can do wonders for a person's self-esteem as well.

As a teenager, it's hard to know what advice is right and what is wrong. We often hear stories or advice that may sound believable but are actually myths. Here's a look at some of the most common teen hygiene myths and the truth behind them.

Shaving Makes Hair Grow Back Faster and Thicker:

This one simply isn't true. The reason why it might seem like your hair grows back thicker and darker after shaving is that when you shave, you are cutting off the tapered ends of each strand of hair. When these ends are removed, the remaining strands appear coarser and darker than before shaving. However, this does not mean that shaving causes more hair to grow back in its place!

Need to Douche or Else They'll Smell:

This myth is false. In fact, douching can be harmful to your body's natural balance of beneficial bacteria and can increase your risk for infection. It can also cause an imbalance in your vagina's pH level, which leads to more discharge and odor. Whenever possible, let nature take its course. Stay away from products like douches that claim they can "clean" or "freshen" up down there!

Greasy Foods Cause Acne:

Eating greasy foods does not cause acne. Your skin produces an oily substance called sebum which helps keep skin healthy, but too much of this oil can lead to clogged pores, which leads to breakouts nothing to do with food! So, while eating greasy foods might contribute to an unhealthy diet (which can influence your skin), it won't necessarily give you acne.

Getting a Tan Will Cure Acne:

When it comes to curing acne, getting a tan won't do the trick! While sun exposure may temporarily dry out pimples on our skin's surface due to the heat from UVB rays (which tans our skin), getting a tan actually makes acne worse in the long run as UV radiation breaks down collagen fibers in our skin, which gives us wrinkles over time AND increases inflammation in our skin cells making breakouts worse!

We often get bombarded with conflicting information about what we should or shouldn't do when it comes to personal hygiene practices. It's important to know the truth, but it's also important to know where to seek out the truth.

The good news is that in this day and age, we have access to an endless amount of information via the Internet. Don't be afraid to do some independent research if you see or hear something that just doesn't seem quite right.

DAILY SHOWERS AND DEODORANT

Daily showers help keep our bodies clean and healthy by washing away germs, dirt, and sweat. Showering regularly also helps prevent body odor caused by bacteria buildup on our skin and can be beneficial for mental health. Many people report feeling calmer and more focused after taking a shower.

Shampoo traps oils, so if you do it too frequently, you may dry your hair out, leaving it prone to breakage.

One common misconception is that you have to wash your hair every single day. For the average person, you only need to wash your hair once every two to three days. Hair naturally produces oil this is called sebum. Shampoo is an emulsifier, working to capture and trap excess oil, dirt, and product residue. You then rinse this out when you clean your hair. Some dirt and oil is necessary and natural since the oils provides a protection barrier and moisturizer for the skin.

It varies by person, but you'll know it's time to wash your hair if you notice an itchy scalp, oil, or flaking due to dirt.

Otherwise, it's perfectly fine to skip a day and only shampoo once every two to three days. However, it's a good idea to wash the rest of your body every day.

To make sure you get in the habit of showering every day, choose a time that works best for you: whether that's in the morning before school or at night before bed and stick with it.

It's not enough just to take a shower. You also need to use deodorant to help control body odor throughout the day.

When applying deodorant, make sure you apply it evenly across both armpits so that your skin stays protected all day long.

Gamechanger:
When choosing a deodorant, look for one that is designed specifically for teens. These products typically contain natural ingredients like aloe vera or tea tree oil and will help keep your body odor under control without irritating your skin.

CHEMICALS IN HYGIENE PRODUCTS

Has anyone ever told you that most of the products on the market have at least one harmful ingredient in them? In recent years big companies that make shampoos and soaps have changed their practices and ingredients list to have more natural products. But still, the harmful ingredients are out there, so you have to be careful!

DO:

YOUR OWN RESEARCH

Google a few companies and find out which ones have commitments to ethical and natural ingredients in their products

CHECK THE INGREDIENTS LIST:

Seriously, read the list! If you can't understand any of the words, then it's probably best to stay away from them. The rule is that if the word is super long and sounds Latin then it is probably a scientific word or a chemical. If there is a bracket right beside the difficult to pronounce word with an English word in it [like lavender] then you're in the clear.

DON'T :

BUY THE CHEAPEST PRODUCT AVAILABLE TO YOU

These will be the products that have the most harmful ingredients. Of course, there will be a time in your life when you can't afford an eleven dollar bottle of shampoo. If that's the case, then you might want to consider recipes for making your own shampoo. Google it!

Some of the most common and dangerous ingredients found in personal care products are sulfates and parabens.

Sulphates are often used as a cleaning agent and can dry out your skin and hair. Parabens act as preservatives and have been linked to hormone disruption and cancer. In addition, you should also look out for phthalates, triclosan, formaldehyde, and synthetic fragrances as these have all been linked to various health issues.

PARABENS

What:
Parabens prevent the growth of mold, bacteria and yeasts. They are added to cosmetics and personal care products to increase shelf-life and stability.

Found In:
Parabens are commonly found in cosmetics and personal care items such as lotions, sunscreen, antiperspirants, makeup and hair products. Parabens may also be found in chewing gum and mouthwash.

Science:
Parabens are endocrine disruptors that can mimic estrogen in the body. Studies show that parabens affect the mechanisms of normal breast cells and influence their abnormal growth, leading to risk for breast cancer.

Top Tips:
Look for products labeled "paraben-free. Common parabens include the suffex paraben or hydroxylbenzoate in the name!

TRICLOSAN

What:
Triclosan is an antimicrobial agent added to a wide array of household and industrial products to prevent the growth of bacteria and fungus.

Found In:
Triclosan is frequently found in liquid antibacterial soaps, toothpastes and cosmetics. It has also been added to clothes, toys, cutting boards, home products and other consumer products.

PHTHALATES

What:
Phthalates, pronounced THAL-ates, are a group of chemicals primarily used to soften and improve the flexibility and durability of plastics, Some phthalates are also used as solvents and stabilizers in product formulations.

Found In:
Phthalates are found in plastics, building materials, cleaning products. insecticides, pharmaceuticals, food packaging, home décor children's toys, and personal care products. They are also used in fragrances.

Science:
Phthalates are endocrine disruptors and may disrupt several hormonal systems in the human body. Evidence links several specific phthalates to breast cancer and other negative health effects.

Top Tips:
Avoid buying personal care products that contain "fragrance" or "perfume." Avoid fragrances and air fresheners. Avoid plastics for food prep and storage. Use glass, ceramic, or metal for food preparation and storage.

Science:
Low levels of triclosan are estrogenic and increase the growth of breast cancer cells that are estrogen-sensitive. At higher levels, triclosan suppresses the growth of these cells. Triclosan may also increase thyroid hormone levels.

Top Tips:
Avoid anti-microbial soaps, toothpastes and other products claiming to be antimicrobial, and avoid those that contain triclosan or 5-chloro-2-(2,4-dichlorophenoxy)phenol. Wash hands with plain soap, not antibacterial.

So, now that you know how potentially harmful these chemicals can be, it's time to start looking for better options! One way is to look for products labeled " or all natural" as they will not contain any of the ingredients.

There are plenty of recipes online for everything from homemade shampoo bars to natural deodorants that don't contain any worrisome chemicals. Plus, making your own beauty products gives you full control over what goes into them. No more worrying about hidden nasties!

SO HOW CLEAN ARE YOU, REALLY?

TAKE THIS HYGIENE QUIZ:

SCAN ME

BRUSHING AND FLOSSING

It's no secret that brushing and flossing are important for your dental health, but why? Brushing helps remove food particles and bacteria from the surfaces of our teeth, which helps prevent plaque buildup. Plaque is a sticky film of bacteria that builds up on teeth over time if not properly removed. Regular brushing prevents this buildup from happening.

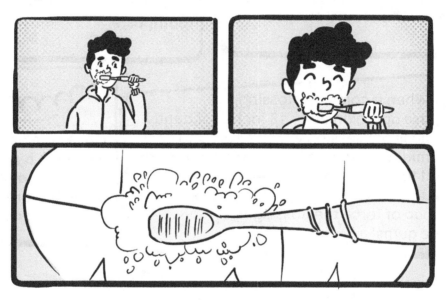

Flossing helps remove plaque from between the teeth that a toothbrush can't reach. This type of plaque can be hazardous because it can lead to gum disease, cavities, and even tooth loss if left untreated. In addition to removing plaque ii flossing also stimulates the gums, which increases blood flow and keeps them healthy.

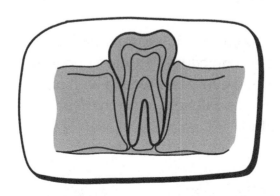

Now that we know why brushing and flossing are important, let's take a look at some tips for proper technique.

 When brushing your teeth, use gentle circular motions along the gum line with an angle bristled toothbrush to help massage the gums. This removes bacteria from all sides of the tooths' surface.

Don't forget to brush your tongue as well. This will help get rid of any remaining food particles or bacteria in your mouth. It's recommended to brush twice a day for two minutes each time using fluoride toothpaste.

When it comes to flossing, use approximately 18 inches of dental floss per session wrapped around each middle finger before threading through two front teeth at a time in an up-and-down motion until reaching the gum line. Be sure not to snap or force the floss against sensitive gums!

Make sure you are thorough by starting with one side of your mouth before working on the other side.

NAIL CARE

Keeping your nails clean is the first step in proper nail care. Use a soft brush or an orange stick dipped in warm water to scrub away dirt and debris from under the nails, being careful not to scratch the skin around them.

You should also keep your cuticles moisturized with a cuticle oil or cream, as dry cuticles can cause irritation and lead to infection. Trim your nails at least once every two weeks with a pair of manicure scissors or clippers: this will help keep them short and prevent splitting and cracking.

SKIN CARE

Your skin has three main layers. The outermost layer is known as the epidermis. This layer provides a natural barrier against water loss and environmental factors such as bacteria.

Underneath the epidermis is the dermis, which contains nerve endings that help to sense touch and temperature and blood vessels that help deliver oxygen and nutrients to cells in the epidermis.

Finally, underneath the dermis is a thick layer of fat that helps insulate your body from cold temperatures.

There are a few common problems that you might notice on your skin, especially as you get older. Moles are small spots on our skin that can be either flat or raised. They usually range in color from light brown to black but can sometimes be pink or flesh colored as well.

Moles can appear anywhere on our body but are most common on areas exposed to the sun like our face, arms, or legs. While most moles are harmless, it's important to keep an eye on them for any changes in size or color because these could be signs of melanoma. (A type of skin cancer).

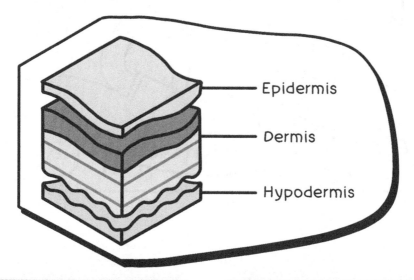

Epidermis

Dermis

Hypodermis

Resting your hands on the face can transfer bacteria onto the skin, which can lead to breakouts. Touching your face can also trigger excess oil production, leading to clogged pores and acne. To keep the skin healthy and clear, keep the hands off the face and avoid picking at breakouts.

And finally, sleep! Sleep is essential for overall health and well being, including the health of our skin. Getting enough sleep helps reduce inflammation, heal and regenerate skin cells, and reduce stress levels. Aim for at least 7 to 9 hours of sleep each night to help maintain healthy skin.

WASHING "THE T ZONE"

As a teenager, taking care of your skin is an important part of developing good life skills. A great place to start is the "T Zone" which includes the forehead, nose, and chin.

To properly wash your T Zone, you should begin with a cleansing routine. This means using a mild cleanser to help remove dirt, oil and other impurities from your pores without too much drying out your skin.

If you have oily or acne prone skin, look for oil free and non-comedogenic cleansers that won't clog up your pores further. You can also try using natural ingredients like honey or yogurt as alternatives to store bought cleansers.

Gamechanger:
Once you've established a regular cleansing routine, you may want to consider adding treatments to target specific issues in your T Zone, such as acne or dryness. For example, spot treatments containing salicylic acid can help reduce inflammation and unclog pores, while hyaluronic acid helps maintain moisture levels in the skin. Serums with antioxidants can also be used to protect from environmental damage caused by pollutants in the air and sun exposure.

FACIAL SHAVING

For most teens, shaving is an important part of developing life skills as they become adults. Although it can be intimidating to pick up a razor for the first time, the basics are very straightforward.

The most important thing when it comes to shaving is choosing the right razor.

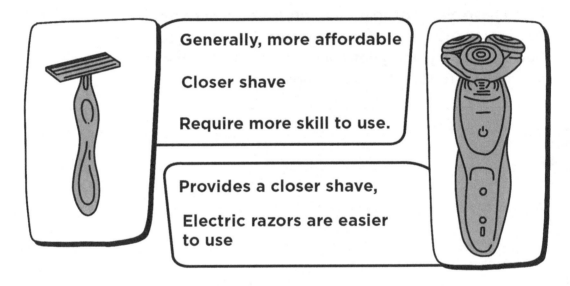

Generally, more affordable

Closer shave

Require more skill to use.

Provides a closer shave,

Electric razors are easier to use

So, consider your needs before deciding on which type of razor you should buy.

Once you have your razor, you'll need to prepare your skin for shaving. Wetting your skin with warm water will soften your hairs and make them easier to cut. Using a pre-shave oil or gel will help protect your skin from irritation and ingrown hairs caused by the razor blade.

Finally, make sure you use a good quality shaving cream or soap. This will help create a protective barrier between your skin and the razor blade while also allowing it to glide smoothly over your skin without any tugging or pulling.

Here are a few more tips that will make your shaving experience better:

Take your time and go slowly.
Shaving too quickly can lead to nicks and cuts on your skin. Not only is this uncomfortable, but it can also increase the risk of infection if not treated properly.

Make sure you shave in the direction that your hair grows (generally downwards) so that you don't irritate or damage your skin further. Going against the grain may seem like it would give you a closer shave, but this is not true in practice and could end up causing more harm than good!

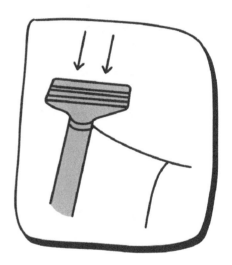

Rinse off any remaining cream or soap after every stroke so that you don't transfer bacteria from one area of skin to another as you shave.

PERIODS

Every month, millions of teenagers go through their first period. It can be a scary and daunting experience, especially if you don't know what to expect or how to manage it. The good news is that with the right information and life skills, managing your period doesn't have to be difficult! Here are a few ideas for how to do this:

Create a routine around your menstrual cycle using a free app like Clue or Flo. This can help you better prepare for when it arrives each month. Try tracking your cycle in a free app like, which will alert you when your period is coming so you can stock up on supplies.

Create a plan for taking care of yourself during your cycle by setting aside time for self-care activities like reading, journaling, exercising, meditating, or doing whatever helps you feel the most relaxed and comfortable. This will help make sure that you have time to take care of yourself during this important part of your life.

Decide which hygiene product works best for you- If the product type that you are using right now makes you uncomfortable, be sure to shop around for an alternative. In the next few pages, we'll be discussing the pros and cons of the various types of hygiene products.

Plan Around It- Don't schedule pool parties, beach days or sporting tournaments near the time of your period.

Emotionally Prepare- If you know that there is something coming up in your schedule that is going to be stressful try to reschedule this. Examples: a job interview, an important talk with your romantic interest, etc. Try not to make any life changing decisions around the time of your period either.

Every Person's body is different, and there is no one size fits all approach when it comes to managing periods.

Gamechanger:
If you're feeling overwhelmed by managing your period or just want additional support from an expert, there are resources available that can help. Consider talking to an adult in your life (like a parent or health provider) who can provide guidance and support as needed. They may also be able to provide you with information on where and how to find free or low cost products like pads and tampons if you're in need.

PERIOD STATISTICS

51
In the U.S., the average age that a woman experiences menopause is 51.

40
The time between a woman's first period and her last is about 40 years.

32
Only 32 percent of women in the U.S. stated they are comfortable talking to female classmates or colleagues about their periods.

800
Most sanitary pads use plastic that requires 800 years to decompose.

HYGIENE PRODUCTS

Some people find that using pads works best for them; others may prefer tampons or menstrual cups. Experiment with different products until you find what works best for you and makes you feel the most comfortable during your cycle.

Item	Cost	Pros	Cons
Pads	$2 – $8 per pack	Easy to use and widely available	Single use so not ideal for the environment
Tampons	$4 – $9	Small and easy to place in your purse. You won't notice that you're wearing one.	Small risk of Toxic Shock Syndrome [see the next page for details]
Menstrual Cups	$35 – $50	Reusable, good for the environment	Can be messy and tricky to use for a beginner.

PADS

These are among the most commonly used feminine sanitary products for their ease of use and safety. They are long strips of cotton padding that stick to your underwear and are designed to soak up the menstrual fluid, which you throw away after each use. Pads should always be disposed of in the garbage and never in toilets.

TAMPONS

These are one time use cotton tubes that are placed inside the vagina to absorb the flow. Depending on the brand, they are designed to be used for up to five hours.

MENSTRUAL CUPS

A 'cup shaped' flexible silicone that is used similarly to a tampon.

TOXIC SHOCK SYNDROME (TSS)

Something that is often not spoken of is the risk of developing Toxic Shock Syndrome when regularly using tampons as your feminine hygiene product of choice. TSS is a serious bacterial condition that can cause damage to your vital organs. If you are a regular user of tampons and have any of these symptoms, be sure to talk with a parent about it and or contact your doctor:

- Fever
- Low blood pressure
- Headache
- Muscle aches
- Confusion
- Diarrhea
- Nausea
- Vomiting
- Rash
- Redness of eyes, mouth, and throat
- Seizures

IS THERE A WAY TO AVOID TSS AND STILL USE TAMPONS?

The tampon product has come a long way since the risk of TSS was first identified. But while it is minimized, the risk is still there. If you know that you still want to use tampons, here are a few pointers:

- Only use tampons while menstruating.

- Leave it in for the recommended time.

- Use the lowest absorbency necessary.

HOW TO GET INTO A GOOD PERSONAL HYGIENE ROUTINE

When you first start developing your personal hygiene routine, it can be overwhelming to think about all the steps that you need to take.

HERE ARE A FEW TIPS:

START SMALL AND FOCUS ON ONE STEP AT A TIME

For example, if you have trouble remembering to brush your teeth, set an alarm for two times a day when you brush your teeth and floss. Setting reminders can help make sure that brushing and flossing become part of your daily routine.

FIND THE PRODUCTS THAT WORK BEST FOR YOU

Everyone's skin type is different, for example, so finding the right soap or face wash is important. Experiment with different products until you find something that works well with your skin type and makes you feel comfortable in your own skin.

CONSIDER ENVIRONMENTAL FACTORS

If you're in an area with hard water, look for products specifically designed for hard water use.

MAKE PERSONAL HYGINE FUN!

Find activities or products that make taking care of yourself enjoyable instead of tedious or boring. Buy yourself a new face mask every month or try out differently scented body washes little things like this can make it easier to stick to a routine and enjoy taking care of yourself more often!

SELF-CARE CHECKLIST

WEEK OFF:

TASKS	S	M	T	W	T	F	S

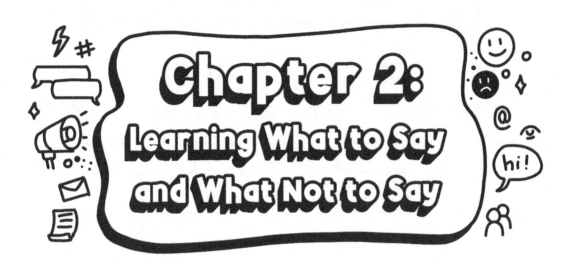

Chapter 2: Learning What to Say and What Not to Say

How you present yourself doesn't just come down to what you look like, it's also about what you say. What people hear from you is just as important as what they see.

We've all been in situations where we regret something we said or did, but have you ever thought about how to avoid similar situations in the future? Learning how to manage your thoughts and words is an important life skill that can help you navigate difficult conversations, avoid embarrassment, and even reduce stress.

Speaking before you think often leads to saying the wrong thing at the wrong time.

I remember once I was talking with a friend of mine about a movie she wanted to see. When she asked me if I wanted to go along with her, my first instinct was to say no. Before I could think it through, though, I blurted out "I don't like movies like that."

Later on, I realized what I said wasn't really true there are plenty of movies that fall into the category she was talking about that I actually enjoy! It just came out wrong because my initial reaction had been to say no without really thinking about it. Unfortunately, my rude response also hurt her feelings, and she didn't ask me if I wanted to see any other movie. The conversation ended.

This is a very minor example, and it was easily rectified. I apologized and we moved on. However, if you don't think before you speak, it could lead to far worse consequences.

It's moments like these when managing your thoughts and words that can be beneficial. It doesn't mean you should stay silent. It just means, rather than speaking without thinking, pause for a moment before responding and give yourself time to process the situation.

This gives you the opportunity to word things more carefully and make sure your response is accurate and appropriate for the situation at hand. You might still decide to say something negative or disagreeable but at least this way you'll be doing so after considering all angles of the conversation instead of just reacting on impulse.

Another way managing your thoughts can be useful is by avoiding unnecessary arguments or debates altogether. Instead of offering up an opinion right away, ask questions. It will show you're interested in understanding the other person better while also giving them a chance to explain their point of view more fully before you share yours.

This allows for more productive conversations and meaningful discussions instead of heated debates that lead nowhere!

CAN YOU THINK OF A TIME WHEN YOU KNOW YOU SHOULD HAVE THOUGHT HARDER ABOUT WHAT TO SAY?
WHAT WAS THE SITUATION?

_____
_____
_____
_____
_____

HOW DID YOU FEEL AFTER SAYING WHAT YOU SAID? AND HOW DO YOU THINK THE LISTENER FELT?

_____
_____
_____
_____
_____

WHAT WOULD YOU DO DIFFERENTLY NEXT TIME?

_____
_____
_____
_____
_____

Putting your foot in your mouth is embarrassing, but it can also have a negative effect on certain relationships or opportunities, such as a job interview. Taking a few moments to pause and consider what you want to say before speaking can help you prevent these kinds of problems.

It's true that words have power. Kind words can uplift peoples' emotions, while harsh or ill considered words can undermine others' self esteem and trust. Being mindful of the impact of your words on other people will help build strong relationships with family members, friends, peers, and colleagues alike.

We've all heard the phrase, "think before you speak." But what does it really mean? It means making an effort to carefully consider the words you use and the impact they will have on others. Taking the time to think before you speak can be a powerful way to shape relationships and make a positive difference in your life.

Thinking about what you say before you say it is important because it allows you to be mindful of how your words might affect other people. It also gives you more control over how you present yourself and your ideas: which can help create positive relationships with those around you.

By taking a moment to pause and reflect on what you want to say, you can craft thoughtful responses that are more likely to be received positively.

HOW DO WORDS MAKE YOU FEEL?

Read over the dialogue pieces below and then circle the feeling that the listener might have after hearing it.

STRATEGIES TO HELP YOU THINK BEFORE YOU SPEAK

It's always a good idea to think before speaking, but there are certain situations where it's especially important. In arguments or disagreements, for example, thinking before speaking can help prevent heated exchanges from escalating further.

It also helps in job interviews or professional meetings, where your ability to express yourself clearly and thoughtfully can often make all the difference between getting the job or not.

THERE ARE A FEW STRATEGIES THAT CAN HELP YOU DO THIS.

The first is to give yourself plenty of time.	Pay close attention to other people's energy.	Decide what to say using 'THINK' (true, helpful, inspiring, necessary, kind).
Before you respond or react to a situation, ask if you can take a few moments to think before saying anything. You don't need to provide an explanation: just politely state that you need some time to consider your response. This allows you to step away from the situation and take a breather, giving your brain time to process the request and come up with an appropriate response.	Look at their body language, tone of voice, and facial expressions—all of which can give insight into how the other person is feeling or what they might be expecting from the conversation. If someone seems uncomfortable or upset, it may be wise to pause and assess how best to proceed before continuing with what was previously discussed.	This is a great way to ensure that what we are about to say aligns with our values and intentions. Going through this checklist can help us decide whether our words will be beneficial for everyone involved or not worth saying at all.

We should always strive for positive conversations that encourage growth and connection rather than negative ones filled with emotionally charged language that can create tension between people.

THREE-STEP DEEP BREATHING METHOD

1. GROUND YOURSELF AND FOCUS ON YOUR BREATH:

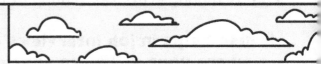

Before your interview begins, find a quiet spot where you can sit down and close your eyes. Ground yourself by placing your feet flat on the floor and resting your hands on your lap. Begin to focus on your breath, noticing the inhale and exhale without any judgment or attempts to change it. Simply observe and focus entirely on the sound and sensation of your breath.

2. SLOW, DEEP BREATHS:

Start taking slow, deep breaths. Inhale through your nose for four counts, filling your chest and abdomen with air. Pause for a moment at the top of the breath before you start to exhale slowly through your mouth for six counts. It's essential to exhale longer than you inhale. This technique not only centers you but also helps in engaging your vagus nerve, which triggers a calming response in your body. Repeat this cycle of inhaling and exhaling at least ten times.

3. VISUALIZE SUCCESS WITH EACH BREATH:

As you perform this deep breathing exercise, start incorporating positive visualizations about your upcoming interview. With each inhale, imagine you are breathing in confidence, and with each exhale, you are releasing any doubts, fears, or anxieties. Picture yourself walking into the interview room with poise, answering questions with ease and confidence, and making an excellent impression on your interviewer. Make sure to keep your visualization positive and focus on the successful outcome you desire.

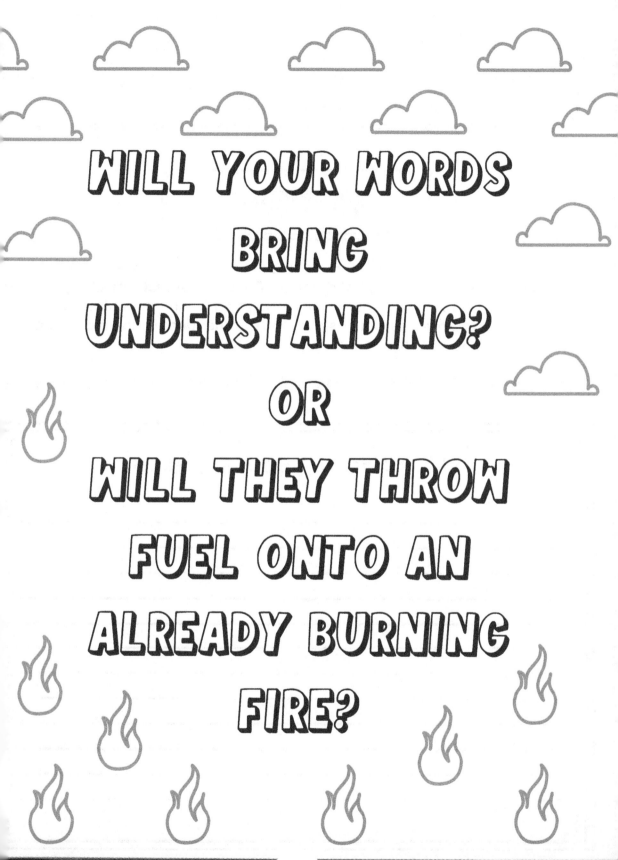

WILL YOUR WORDS BRING UNDERSTANDING? OR WILL THEY THROW FUEL ONTO AN ALREADY BURNING FIRE?

ROLE MODELS

Most of us can think of one or two people in our life who speak in a respectful and kind way most of the time. These individuals are likely role models in your life, people that you look up to and want to emulate or copy. They present themselves in a positive way to other people and make good impressions wherever they go.

Take some time to think about what makes them different than the people who aren't very good at this.

WRITE YOUR THOUGHTS HERE:

_____

_____

_____

_____

_____

_____

_____

_____

_____

_____

_____

_____

_____

DRAW A PICTURE OF YOUR ROLE MODEL[S] SPEAKING TO OTHERS.

TIP: Remember to include details of how they present themselves, their facial expression, and their body language.

WHAT TECHNIQUES DO YOU THINK THEY USE TO ENSURE THAT WHAT THEY SAY IS POSITIVE, KIND, AND THOUGHTFUL?

_____
_____
_____
_____
_____
_____
_____
_____

INSPIRED? GOT SOME NEW iDEAS?

List some techniques that you think would help you to think before you speak:

_____

_____

_____

_____

_____

_____

_____

_____

_____

_____

_____

Gamechanger:

Thinking something doesn't necessarily mean we should say it. In fact, often, reflecting silently on thoughts or feelings without verbalizing them can create more meaningful interactions without damaging relationships.

Here's an exercise you can try.

Instead of speaking up impulsively, try pondering something first: sometimes, silence speaks louder than words. We've included an activity for you to try to practice this behavior below.
Later, we'll tell you more about how this can lead to better self-care and overall mental health. After all, if you don't take care of yourself, you can't do anything for others.

TRY THIS!

Imagine that someone has said something hurtful or mean to you.
How would you respond? Take a few moments to think about this.

NOW WRITE DOWN YOUR INITIAL RESPONSE. MAKE SURE TO INCLUDE ANY EMOTIONS YOU FELT IN THE MOMENT AS WELL.

_____
_____
_____
_____
_____
_____

Once you have written it down, take some time to reflect on how this response might come across to others. Could it be seen as disrespectful or rude? Is there a better way for you to express your feelings without seeming too harsh?

NOW, RE-WRITE YOUR RESPONSE USING MORE THOUGHTFUL LANGUAGE THAT CONVEYS YOUR MESSAGE WITHOUT BEING TOO AGGRESSIVE OR UNKIND. FOCUS ON USING LANGUAGE THAT WILL ENCOURAGE UNDERSTANDING AND RESPECT FROM BOTH PARTIES INVOLVED EVEN IF THE OTHER PERSON DOES NOT AGREE WITH WHAT YOU HAVE SAID.

_____
_____
_____
_____
_____
_____

Remember, this exercise isn't just about learning how to respond in difficult situations; it's also about communicating in a way that shows respect for yourself, as well as everyone around you.

Finally, practice responding out loud with new words or phrases that express your thoughts more clearly and effectively. Find different ways of expressing yourself so that you become comfortable with articulating your feelings especially if they are difficult ones.

This will help build confidence when communicating with others, which can have positive long term effects on relationships and self esteem!

In the digital age, it's easy to react impulsively to things. We have so much access to information and what feels like an endless number of opinions, making it hard to know how to respond in any given situation. But the truth is that sometimes, silence speaks louder than words.

Pausing before speaking allows us time for reflection. What do I really want? What are my goals here? How will this affect me in the long run? Thinking through situations helps build problem solving skills to better manage difficult conversations and make decisions that align with our values and goals in life.

In the next chapter, we'll take a closer look at how self-care and mental health comes into play. How do they affect how we deal with our relationships with others, as well as our relationship with ourselves?

Chapter 3: Self Care & Mental Health

Taking care of your mental health is an important part of life, especially as a teen. With the ever changing pressures of school, family, and friends, it can be hard to take time for yourself. That said, maintaining good mental health is essential for teens to thrive emotionally and intellectually during these formative years.

While there's no substitute for formal mental health care from a licensed professional, there are simple steps you can follow to advocate for yourself and follow a good self care routine.

Self-care is a vital part of one's mental health and well being, especially during the teenage years. It can be defined as any activity that we do deliberately to take care of our physical, mental, and emotional health.

The idea behind self-care is simple: focus on yourself and do whatever it takes to feel better whether it be taking a walk, reading a book, or just taking some time for yourself. Teenagers often struggle with finding a balance between school and life responsibilities, making selfcare even more important in their lives.

See Reality as It Is

Life isn't always perfect, and there will be times when things don't go our way. It's important to learn how to accept reality as it is instead of focusing on what could have been or what could be. This allows us to move past disappointment and focus on solutions instead of dwelling on the problem itself.

Focus on Having a Few, but True, Friendships

WE OFTEN FEEL PRESSURE TO FIT IN WITH LARGE GROUPS, BUT THIS CAN ACTUALLY BE DETRIMENTAL IF WE DON'T TAKE TIME OUT FOR OURSELVES TOO. BELOW, WRITE DOWN A FEW TRAITS THAT YOU TREASURE MOST IN YOUR FRIENDSHIPS:

_____
_____
_____
_____
_____

NOW ASK YOURSELF. DO THE FRIENDS YOU HAVE IN YOUR LIFE REFLECT THOSE TRAITS?

_____
_____
_____
_____
_____

Gamechanger:

Instead of trying to please everyone, focus on having a few true friends who genuinely care about you and make time for them regularly! This will help cultivate meaningful relationships while allowing you some "me time" which is essential for good mental health.

PRACTICE POSITIVE SELF-TALK

We all make mistakes, and when we do, it's easy to beat ourselves up about it or dwell on our failures too much.

Instead, use positive self talk as a way of building up your confidence again by reminding yourself that even though mistakes were made, there are steps you can take to fix them or do better next time.

HERE ARE SOME POSITIVE AFFIRMATIONS YOU CAN USE WHEN YOU'RE IN A PINCH:

1. "I deserve to be happy."

2. "I have the power to be happy no matter the circumstance."

3. "I accept all the good that is in my life."

4. "I have a positive outlook no matter the situation."

5. "I have many reasons to smile."

6. "I am joyous about my opportunities."

7. "I am grateful for everything I have in my life".

TRY MEDITATION OR YOGA

Meditation has been proven to reduce stress and improve focus. So, you can see how it's great while you're stressing over exams! Later, I'll give you more information on how to use meditation for a calmer life.

Yoga is another great option! Not only does yoga help reduce tension levels, but it also helps increase flexibility and mobility. This can help keep injuries at bay during physical activities like sports.

Gamechanger:
If you can, take your meditation outside. Being surrounded by nature helps reduce stress levels while also providing a calming atmosphere in which you can relax and unwind after a long day at school.

DON'T BE AFRAID OF CREATIVE EXPRESSION

CREATIVE EXPRESSION CAN HELP RELEASE SOME OF THE BUILT UP EMOTIONS FROM DAY TO DAY LIFE, SUCH AS ANGER OR FRUSTRATION, THROUGH OUTLETS LIKE DRAWING, WRITING STORIES/POEMS, PLAYING MUSIC, ETC., WHAT ARE SOME OF YOUR FAVORITE WAYS TO EXPRESS YOURSELF?

_____
_____
_____
_____
_____

WHEN WAS THE LAST TIME YOU DEVOTED TIME TO CREATIVITY?

_____
_____
_____
_____
_____
_____

PURSUE HOBBIES

Even if you don't consider yourself creative, everyone has at least one hobby. Hobbies are a great way to boost your mental health. Just think, you're doing something you enjoy and know that you're good at. And everyone needs that!

Whether it's playing an instrument, taking apart an engine of a car, acting in a play, or playing a sport hobbies allow you to have a breather from the responsibilities you have at home and school and allow for much needed social interactions as well.

_____

_____

_____

_____

_____

_____

FIND HAPPINESS IN SMALL THINGS

We all have days when we don't feel our best but taking a moment to appreciate the small joys throughout your day can help keep your spirits up!

One way simple and easy way you can do this is by taking time to savor a delicious snack! Even just taking the time to appreciate the beauty of nature can make all the difference in how you feel about your day and yourself.

CIRCLE THE 'SMALL THINGS IN LIFE THAT REALLY BRING YOU JOY:

Walking my dog first thing in the morning.

Reading my favorite book before I go to bed.

Relaxing in the tub with some candles and spa music playing.

Playing sports with my friends.

Going for a leisurely drive in the countryside.

Sipping a cappuccino and eating a gourmet pastry at a local cafe.

START A PRACTICE OF GRATITUDE

On a similar note, gratitude is simply being thankful for what you have in life, which helps us focus on the positive rather than worrying about things that we cannot change or control.

Take some time each day to think of three things that you're grateful for. This could be anything from having good friends or family members who care about you, or even just being able to enjoy a beautiful sunset.

Get started with this exercise today!

LIST A FEW OF THE THINGS YOU'RE THANKFUL FOR TODAY:

_____

_____

_____

_____

_____

TAKE THIS BOOK AND LOOK OUT YOUR NEAREST WINDOW. WHAT DO YOU SEE THAT YOU CAN BE GRATEFUL FOR? WRITE IT DOWN HERE:

_____

_____

_____

_____

_____

NOW SIT DOWN IN A COMFORTABLE PLACE IN YOUR BEDROOM AND CLOSE YOUR EYES. FOCUS ON YOUR FOUR SENSES. WHAT DO YOU HEAR, SMELL, TASTE, AND FEEL? OF THOSE, WHAT CAN YOU BE GRATEFUL FOR?
[for example, you might hear the sound of your brother talking to your mom.]

_____

_____

_____

_____

WHAT DO YOU OFTEN TAKE FOR GRANTED ABOUT YOUR LIFE? AND HOW CAN YOU STOP THAT BAD HABIT TODAY?

_____
_____
_____
_____
_____
_____

IF YOU HAVE ANY OTHER THOUGHTS ABOUT DEVELOPING A PRACTICE OF GRATITUDE, WRITE THEM HERE:

_____
_____
_____
_____
_____
_____
_____
_____
_____
_____
_____
_____
_____
_____
_____
_____
_____
_____
_____

TURN OFF YOUR PHONE FOR A FEW HOURS A DAY

Staring at screens all day isn't healthy for anyone, especially teens who are still developing cognitively and emotionally! Set aside some time each day (an hour at least) when you turn off your phone and step away from social media so that you can focus on more meaningful activities like reading books, talking with friends face to face, and going outside for a walk or run.

DO SOMETHING KIND FOR SOMEONE ELSE

One of the best ways to practice self-care is by doing something kind for someone else. This could be as simple as writing a nice note or sending an encouraging text message to a friend or family member.

Doing good deeds helps us feel connected to our community, providing us with a sense of purpose and satisfaction. Plus, it's always nice to spread positivity! Can't think of any kind things you can do?

Here's a list to get you started:

1. Pay for someone's meal or drink at a restaurant or coffee shop.
2. Leave a kind note or uplifting message for someone to find.
3. Help a stranger with their groceries or offer to carry their heavy bags.
4. Hold the door open for someone and greet them with a smile.
5. Offer to pick up groceries or run errands for an elderly neighbor or someone who is sick.
6. Donate to a charity or volunteer your time at a local organization.
7. Compliment a stranger or tell them they are doing a good job.
8. Offer to babysit for free for a single parent or couple who needs a night out.
9. Bring a treat or small gift to a friend or co-worker just because.
10. Simply listen and be there for someone who needs to talk or vent.

START A DAILY ROUTINE AND FOLLOW IT

When life gets busy, it can be difficult to stay organized and on top of things. That's why having a daily routine is so important! Having a structured schedule will help keep you accountable and ensure that you're making time for your self each day.

I'll give you more details on how to incorporate a routine into your life in the next chapter.

GET ENOUGH SLEEP

Adequate sleep is essential for feeling rested and restored each day; however, this isn't always easy. Again, I'll give you some sleep tips later, but for now, know that this is a crucial part of self-care.

WATCH YOUR BREATHING

Taking deep breaths helps reduce stress levels by allowing oxygen to flow through our bodies more easily. This is especially helpful when we start feeling overwhelmed by our emotions or the tasks at hand.

Gamechanger:
Whenever possible, take deep breaths throughout the day. Inhale deeply through your nose while counting to ten, then exhale slowly through your mouth while counting again to clear your head and re-center yourself.

CHECK IN WITH YOURSELF OFTEN

Lastly, it's important to check in with your self regularly throughout the day (not just once at night!). Ask yourself how you're feeling emotionally. If something doesn't feel right, then take action before things get worse.

1. Am I using my time wisely?

2. Am I taking anything for granted?

3. Am I employing a healthy perspective?

4. Am I living true to myself?

5. Am I waking up in the morning ready to take on the day?

6. Am I thinking negative thoughts before I fall asleep?

7. Am I putting enough effort into my relationships?

8. Am I taking care of myself physically?

9. Am I letting matters that are out of my control stress me out?

10. Am I achieving the goals that I've set for myself?

Self-care and ensuring your mental health are important steps in becoming a mature adult. If you've ever flown on a plane, you know the safety instructions that dictate that you should put on your own oxygen mask before helping others with theirs. The same goes for good self-care. If you're not in a good mental state yourself, you can't do anything for anyone else. Self care isn't self ish it's vital!

A crucial component of good self-care is setting yourself up for success with a solid and predictable routine. A routine will allow you to take much of the guesswork out of your day for more seamless transitions and increased productivity. Everything will just feel easier!

In the next chapter, we'll take a closer look at how to set up a routine so you can do just that.

Chapter 4:
Set Your Routine

Routines provide clarity and consistency in your life, which can help improve your mental health. Having a plan for the day gives you something to focus on and reduces stress when it comes to making decisions about what to do next.

When I was in high school, I was the kind of person who thought that having a routine would make me boring. So, when it came to managing my time, I was all over the place. I rarely kept up with my homework or assignments and often forgot about upcoming tests and quizzes.

As you can imagine, this made life pretty stressful and caused me to feel overwhelmed much of the time. It wasn't until later on that I realized that having a consistent routine is actually one of the keys to success.

As I mentioned earlier, routines can be incredibly helpful for teenagers, especially when they are trying to develop a sense of independence and organization. Having a routine helps you stay on track with your goals, be more productive, and give structure to your day.

Routines also help with goal setting by providing a timetable for work or study that helps you stay on track and make progress toward the things that are important to you. And believe it or not, this life skill [more than many other ones] will help make you feel ready for college, your career and managing a household and family one day, because as much as adults don't like it, schedules do rule the world. The faster you get yourself on a schedule and used to it, the easier your future will be.

When establishing a routine, it's important to set realistic goals and expectations that fit into your lifestyle. That means when you are structuring your schedule be sure to give yourself enough time to adjust physically, emotionally, and mentally adjust to the next task. We'll talk about more tips and tricks in a second, but first, let's establish what your current routine looks like:

DAILY PLANNER

SCHEDULE

06:00	
07:00	
08:00	
09:00	
10:00	
11:00	
12:00	
13:00	
14:00	
15:00	
16:00	
17:00	
18:00	
19:00	
20:00	
21:00	
22:00	

TOP PRIORITIES

TO DO LIST

NOTES

SO, HOW DO I START?

Start with the basics, such as setting up an alarm so that you maintain consistent sleep/wake times, and then move on from there. Aim to establish morning, evening, after school, weekend, and school holiday routines so that you have an overall plan in place no matter the situation.

Start Small

Start small by adding a few simple habits to your daily routine that you know you can stick with. This might mean setting an alarm and getting out of bed right away each morning, taking a five minute break in the middle of your homework session to relax and refocus, or drinking a glass of water after lunch every day.

BUILD A ROUTINE THAT WILL STICK

One that is resilient to changes in your school and work schedules

As a teen, it's likely that your school or work schedule will change from semester to semester or job to job as your responsibilities evolve. When creating your routine, make sure that it can be adjusted if needed so that when changes come up, you don't feel overwhelmed or flustered. Being flexible is key!

Write it Down

Writing down your daily routine may seem old fashioned, but it works! Seeing what needs to be done written out on paper can help alleviate stress because it gives you a clear picture of all the tasks you need to accomplish during the day. Plus, crossing off items as they are completed will give you an extra sense of satisfaction!

There are a few different ways you can write down your routine. Here are some examples: Write individual tasks on sticky notes and put them in places you know you'll see them. Write one master list and pin it to your wall or on your homework desk Create a spreadsheet on your computer.

Make it Visual

If writing lists isn't really your thing, try making visual reminders instead.

You could use pictures or colors next to each task so that you know exactly what needs to be done without having to read through everything all over again.

For example, if you have an assignment due tomorrow, make sure there is something on your list that stands out, like using red ink or putting a star next to its name so that it pops out from all the other items on your list.

Gamechanger:
If physical reminders don't work for you, try digitizing your routine instead. There are lots of apps available (e.g., Google Calendar) which allow users to set reminders for themselves about upcoming deadlines and events, which can help keep them organized and motivated throughout the day.

HERE'S A LIST OF APPS THAT CAN HELP YOU CREATE A DAILY ROUTINE AND HOLD YOU ACCOUNTABLE TO IT:

HABITBULL   TODOIST   FOREST

1. HabitBull:

This app helps you track and monitor your habits over time so that it can give insights into how successful your routines have been. It also provides helpful reminders to help keep you on track with your goals. Additionally, it has an interesting "streak feature that awards points when you meet certain milestones as part of your routine. This app is especially useful if you need motivation and accountability to stay on top of your daily tasks and goals.

2. ToDoist:

This is one of the most popular task management apps out there. It allows users to manage and organize their tasks with features such as priority levels, colour coding, due dates, labels, and project management tools. The app also integrates with various other calendar programs like Google Calendar or Outlook so that users can easily sync up their activities across multiple platforms. It even has a neat "Karma Score which grows as users complete tasks on time!

3. Forest

If staying focused is one of your main issues, then Forest may be the perfect app for you. This unique app encourages users to stay away from their phones while they focus on completing tasks by allowing them to "grow trees" in their virtual forest over time as they stay off their devices for longer periods of time. Plus, the money made from purchases in the app goes towards planting real trees around the world - so it's a win-win!

Be Clear About What Your Free Time Looks Like

Before you start scheduling out every hour of the day, take some time to brainstorm what free time looks like for you. This could include anything from catching up with friends over the phone or taking an online yoga class. Be sure to balance your work time with your free time so that you don't become overwhelmed and then throw out your routine altogether. Choose a few activities that you know bring you joy and make them part of your routine, then you'll have something to look forward to throughout the day.

_____
_____
_____
_____
_____
_____

WRITE DOWN DEADLINES WITHIN YOUR ROUTINE

It's easy to forget one important task when you have multiple deadlines coming at once. To stay organized and on top of things, write down each deadline in your planner or calendar so that you don't miss any important events or assignments.

This way, you won't have any surprises when it comes time for exams or presentations plus, it will help keep your stress levels low.

SCHEDULE EVERYTHING, INCLUDING MEALTIMES AND BEDTIMES

Creating a routine isn't just about doing more work; it's also about making sure that you're taking care of yourself (both mentally and physically).

Be sure to schedule regular mealtimes throughout the day so that you're getting enough fuel for all your busy activities this includes breakfast.

Similarly, set aside specific bedtimes that allow for plenty of restful sleep each night no more late nights cramming for tests!

This will likely require some communication with other members of your family who coordinate meal planning, cooking, and other family events. Or maybe you only have one bathroom in your house, so you need to coordinate with the five other family members to schedule your daily shower.

NAME A FEW ITEMS ON YOUR ROUTINE THAT YOU'LL HAVE TO CHECK IN WITH YOUR FAMILY MEMBERS FOR.
INDICATE WHAT THE ITEM IS AND WHOM YOU'LL NEED TO SPEAK WITH.

_____
_____
_____
_____
_____
_____

Be Patient With Yourself as You Make Your Routine a Habit

It takes time to adjust to any new habit, especially one as comprehensive as creating an effective daily routine.

Don't be too hard on yourself if things don't go according to plan the first few times around; Rome wasn't built in a day!

Your routines should always be evolving according to current needs. If something isn't working, don't be afraid to scrap it entirely or replace it with something else.

If something doesn't feel right or isn't proving useful anymore, don't be afraid to change it up!

LET'S BE PROACTIVE.

WHAT ARE SOME THINGS THAT YOU THINK ARE GOING TO GET IN THE WAY OF YOU FOLLOWING YOUR ROUTINE?

_____
_____
_____
_____
_____
_____

HOW CAN YOU MAKE THIS EASIER FOR YOURSELF?

DAILY ROUTINE

Time	M	T	W	T	F	S	S	TASK
MORNING								
AFTERNOON								
EVENING								
BEFORE BED								

It's easy to see why routines are so important. They provide structure and organization that helps us stay on track with the things we want to accomplish. Routines also give us a sense of stability and well being.

With a routine in place, it becomes easier to take care of your mental health as well as your physical health. In addition, it can provide an opportunity to stay connected with people who matter most in our lives.

To make the most of these benefits, it is important to remain flexible and willing to use different strategies when necessary, so that you can stay on top of your tasks and responsibilities while working towards long term goals.

Now that we understand how routines can benefit our lives, let's move onto taking care of your body! By following a consistent schedule for sleeping, eating, exercising and more, you can be sure you are on the path to greater well being and satisfaction in life.

Let's dive in.

Chapter 5: Taking Care of Your Body

When I was a teenager, I thought I was invincible. I stayed up late into the night, barely slept enough, and ate whatever junk food was around. To be honest, looking back on it now, I had no idea how my body could handle all that abuse—but it did.

That is until one day when my health caught up with me - and suddenly I was dealing with consequences that felt like they were being thrown at me from out of nowhere. I had stomach cramps, dull-looking hair, and other issues I really didn't want to deal with.

It made me realize that taking care of my body isn't something I should put off until later in life—it's an essential life skill that we all need to master as soon as possible.

I've told you a lot so far about how to present yourself in an appealing way whether it's caring for your own mental health, your personal hygiene, or even developing a routine that you can follow each and every day, there are lots of steps you can follow to make sure this happens.

However, it's important to recognize that a great outward appearance starts internally. Before you can think about how to portray yourself to the outside world, you need to make sure your physical health is taken care of.

GET ADEQUATE SLEEP

It's no secret that teenagers need more sleep than adults.

But why is adequate sleep so important?

Sleep plays a critical role in thinking and academic achievement, emotional health, physical health and development, decision making, and even accident prevention. Yet, despite its importance, many of us aren't getting enough of it.

In general, one of the biggest reasons many teens don't get enough sleep is their delayed sleep schedule (also known as circadian rhythm). During adolescence, natural melatonin production shifts later in the evening, meaning you naturally feel sleepy later at night than other people but you still have to wake up early in the morning for school.

To make matters worse, most schools start earlier than recommended by the American Academy of Pediatrics (which suggests 8:30 am or later). This mismatch between teen biology and school schedules leaves many of us struggling with chronic sleep deprivation.

DEFINITION OF CIRCADIAN RHYTHM : CIRCADIAN RHYTHMS ARE PHYSICAL, MENTAL, AND BEHAVIORAL CHANGES THAT FOLLOW A 24 HOUR CYCLE.

Another major factor contributing to poor sleep habits among teens is their use of electronic devices such as smartphones, tablets, and laptops late into the night. Not only does this make it difficult to wind down after a long day, but blue light from screens can also suppress melatonin production which makes falling asleep even harder!

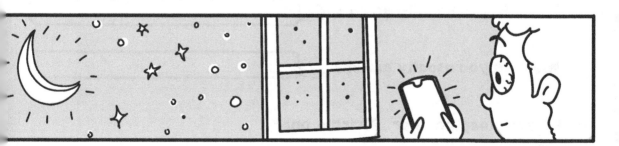

On top of that, the time demands associated with extracurricular activities can also lead to late nights and early mornings.

Finally, mental health conditions like depression or anxiety can play a role in poor sleep habits as well as neurodevelopmental disorders such as Attention Deficit Hyperactivity Disorder (ADHD) For those struggling with these issues, developing healthy sleeping patterns can be even more challenging than usual.

Definition of ADHD:
Short for attention deficit/hyperactivity disorder, ADHD is a condition that is marked by an ongoing pattern of inattention and/or hyperactivity impulsivity that interferes with functioning or development.

THE SLEEP TEST

FIRST OFF, HOW WOULD YOU RATE YOUR SLEEP?

☆ ☆ ☆ ☆ ☆ ☆ ☆ ☆ ☆ ☆

When do you usually go to bed?

When do you usually get up?

Do you sleep on your...?[circle one]

 BACK   SIDE    STOMACH    OTHER

Do you wake up in the middle of the night? {y/n}. # of times

DO YOU OFTEN FEEL ANXIOUS BEFORE GOING TO SLEEP? IF YES, ABOUT WHAT?

_____
_____
_____
_____
_____

HOW DO YOU USUALLY FEEL WHEN YOU WAKE UP?

_____
_____
_____
_____
_____

IF YOU ANSWERED, NOT SO GOOD, THEN OF ALL THE BARRIERS TO SLEEP THAT WE
MENTIONED, WHICH ONES DO YOU THINK ARE AFFECTING YOU?

_____
_____
_____
_____
_____

DRAW A PICTURE OF THE VIBE ' THAT YOU GIVE OFF EACH MORNING RIGHT AFTER YOU WAKE UP:

Now that you have a better idea of your sleep health, here are some simple strategies that we can all implement to get better quality shut eye each night. Let's take a closer look.

HOW MANY HOURS OF SLEEP DO I NEED?

The National Sleep Foundation recommends that teenagers aged 14-17 get 8-10 hours of sleep each night.

RECOMMENDED HOURS OF SLEEP

12-16 hours of sleep	11-14 hours of sleep	10-13 hours of sleep	9-12 hours of sleep	8-10 hours of sleep	7+ hours of sleep
INFANT 4-12 MONTHS	TODDLER 1-2 YEARS	PRE SCHOOL 3-5 YEARS	SCHOOL AGE 6-12 YEARS	TEEN 13-18 YEARS	ADULT 18+ YEARS

That might sound like a lot especially when you factor in all the other things that fill your day but it's essential to make sure you are getting enough restful sleep.

It's also important to note that getting too much sleep (more than 11 hours per night) can also wreak havoc on your body's systems with similar consequences. Sleeping for excessive amounts of time during the day may interfere with nighttime sleeping patterns, leading to insomnia or other sleeping disorders.

Budget Eight Hours of Sleep Into Your Schedule

The first step in establishing a good sleep routine is making sure you have enough time for it! You should budget eight hours into your schedule each night for sleeping. This means having an idea of when you need to go to bed to wake up at the time that works best for your schedule.

For example, if you need to wake up at 7 am each morning, then you should make sure you are in bed by 11 pm the night before.

What Changes Do You Need To Make To Ensure You Get 8 Hours of Sleep?

_____

_____

_____

_____

_____

_____

Stick To The Plan Even On Weekends And Weekdays

It can be tempting on weekends or days off school or work to stay up late and stay in bed late as well.

However, consistency is key when it comes to developing a good sleep routine, which means sticking close to your regular bedtime and wake up time even on days when your schedule isn't full. Doing this will help keep your internal clock (or circadian rhythm) running smoothly so that your body knows when it is time for sleep every day.

Avoid Caffeine in the Afternoon

Another way to develop a good sleep routine is to avoid caffeine after lunchtime or in the afternoon especially if you have trouble falling asleep at night! Caffeine can take several hours after consumption before its effects wear off, so drinking coffee or soda too close to bedtime can leave you feeling wide awake when all you want is some shut eye.

> **Gamechanger:**
> Try cutting out caffeine after lunchtime. This will give your body plenty of time before bedtime for any caffeine still lingering in your system so that it won't interfere with getting a good night's rest.

As a teenager, chances are you've already encountered caffeine. It's found in coffee, tea, energy drinks, and sodas even chocolate has trace amounts of it. But what does caffeine do to your body?

The main ingredient in caffeine is a methylxanthine, which acts as a mild stimulant by blocking adenosine receptors in the brain. Adenosine is a neurotransmitter that helps us relax and get ready for sleep. When caffeine blocks these receptors, it can make us feel more alert and energized. This increased alertness can be helpful when studying or working late at night, but too much caffeine can lead to insomnia and other sleep disturbances if consumed too close to bedtime.

Caffeine also stimulates our cardiovascular system by increasing heart rate and blood pressure, which can be beneficial during exercise or other physical activities. However, drinking too much of it on an ongoing basis could have negative effects on your h eart health over time.

Keep in mind that while having an occasional caffeinated beverage isn't likely to cause any harm, excessive consumption of any type of stimulant should be avoided whenever possible.

COFFEE......COFFEE....COFFEE....

Finally, caffeine has been linked to improved concentration and mental performance due to its ability to increase dopamine levels in the brain. Dopamine is a neurotransmitter associated with motivation, focus and memory all important aspects of learning and productivity.

Again, moderation is key. Consuming too much caffeine may impair mental performance due to feelings of anxiety or jitteriness caused by its stimulating effects on the central nervous system.

How many cups of coffee do you have a day?

What do you take in your coffee?

How late in the day is your last cup?

What affects do you feel from coffee?

CREATE A PRE-BED ROUTINE

Having a pre-bed routine can also be very helpful when trying to establish a good sleep routine. This could include taking a hot bath or shower right before going to bed, reading a book, writing down any worries or thoughts that might be keeping you up, meditating for five minutes...the list goes on!

Gamechanger:
Find something calming that helps clear your mind and prepares you for going asleep --- do this every night around the same time and soon enough it will become second nature.

☐ PUT YOUR PHONE AWAY A HALF AN HOUR BEFORE BED

Using phones and other devices right before bed can disrupt your internal clock and affect your ability to fall asleep. Try putting away all electronics at least half an hour before bedtime so that you can start winding down.

☐ KEEP YOUR BEDROOM COOL, DARK, AND QUIET

Your bedroom should be cool (around 65-67 degrees Fahrenheit), dark, and quiet for your body to relax and enter its natural sleep cycle. Try blackout curtains or an eye mask if there is too much light coming in from outside or from electronic devices in your room.

☐ USE YOUR BED ONLY FOR SLEEP

Most people have trouble sleeping when their bed becomes associated with activities other than sleeping, like studying or watching TV. Make sure that your bed is used only for sleeping so that it becomes a place where you associate relaxation rather than stress.

☐ MOVE THE CLOCK

Watching time pass while lying in bed can cause anxiety which makes it harder for some people to fall asleep quickly! If this happens to you, then try moving the clock away from your line of vision so that it's not easy to see how long it takes for you to fall asleep each night.

☐ BE MINDFUL OF YOUR NAPS

Most people have trouble sleeping when their bed becomes associated with activities other than sleeping, like studying or watching TV. Make sure that your bed is used only for sleeping so that it becomes a place where you associate relaxation rather than stress.

☐ AVOID STIMULATING ACTIVITIES BEFORE BED

Stimulating activities like texting or playing video games can make it harder to fall asleep when bedtime rolls around, as they activate the parts of your brain that should be winding down to get ready for bed.

Instead of engaging in these activities right before bedtime, opt for something more calming like reading a book or listening to some relaxing music.

KEEP A SLEEP DIARY

Keeping track of how much sleep you're getting every night can be helpful in making sure that you're staying on track with healthy sleeping habits. Make note of any naps or changes in sleeping patterns so that if there are any issues with your sleep schedule, they can be identified easily.

HERE'S AN EXAMPLE:

Date	Bedtime	Wake Time	Nighttime Routine	Did I wake Feeling Rested?	Notes

SLEEP DIARY

MINDFULNESS/ MEDITATION

Taking care of yourself is an important part of life, and it can be hard to remember to do sometimes. One way to help yourself stay on track is by incorporating mindfulness and meditation into your daily routine. By taking a few moments each day to focus on yourself, your mental and physical health will benefit greatly.

When we feel overwhelmed or stressed, our bodies tend to tense up, which can affect our physical health in the long run. To counteract this, regular deep breathing exercises, a key element of mindfulness and meditation, can help relax the body and provide relief from stress related tension. Deep breathing also helps bring oxygen into the bloodstream more efficiently, providing more energy throughout the day.

OVERWHELMED OR STRESSED → TENSE UP → AFFECT PHYSICAL HEALTH

RELIEF FROM

OXYGEN + ENERGY

HEAL

RELAX

MEDITATION

DEEP BREATHING EXERCISE

Mindfulness and meditation can also be beneficial for mental health. Taking the time to focus on yourself enables you to check in with your emotions and become aware of what is happening in your mind. This awareness allows you to identify patterns of thought so that when situations arise that make you feel uncomfortable or anxious, you have better tools at hand to manage them effectively.

MINDFULNESS IS THE PRACTICE OF BEING AWARE OF YOUR THOUGHTS, FEELINGS, AND ENVIRONMENT IN THE PRESENT MOMENT WITHOUT JUDGMENT OR CRITICISM.

The benefits of practicing mindfulness and meditation for teens are numerous.
Here are just a few:

1. Mindfulness can reduce stressors and anxiety. Studies have shown that it can improve attentional capacity, increase self-control and compassion toward oneself, improve school behavior, as well as reduce bullying among teens.

2. Mindfulness also encourages better emotion regulation which helps teens replace negative thoughts with more positive ones.

3. Mindfulness can improve your ability to be focused and dedicated to a task. One of the reasons for this is because it takes consistency and dedication to stay on track with your mindfulness routine that you create for yourself.

> ### Gamechanger:
> Some experts recommend dedicating 10-15 minutes twice a day to mindfulness or meditation, but any amount of time spent practicing mindfulness could be beneficial.

Keep in mind that developing this habit takes time as with any skill or hobby so don't expect perfection right away.

NOT SURE HOW TO GET STARTED?

Starting a meditation or mindfulness program is easier than you may think! Here are some tips:

1) Start Small. Consider it your goal to spend five minutes a day on your new practice. You can increase it by a few minutes per day, but only once you've set up your daily routine.

2) Find a Quiet Space where you can focus.

3) Be Consistent but Kind: Do your best to stay on track with your routine, practicing some form of mindfulness every day. But at the same time, be kind to yourself if you miss one day.

4) Use an App to Track Your Mindfulness Routine: There are tons of apps available that can help you to track your mindfulness routine and set up reminders in case you forget.

Gamechanger:
If you choose to meditate indoors, selecting calming background noise may help you focus on your breath or mantra. Some popular choices are guided meditation audio tracks or calming music. You can also try natural soundscapes like rainstorms or ocean waves if they help you relax more.

EXPERIMENT WITH DIFFERENT METHODS OF MEDITATION

There are a few different types of meditation.
We'll break them down for you below.

"THOUGHT HUNTER" METHOD	Instead of trying to push away intrusive thoughts as soon as they come up, acknowledge them, and simply let them pass without judgment. This practice helps us stay in the present moment while being mindful of our thoughts but not getting attached to them.
COUNTING MEDITATION	Start by counting each inhale and exhale until you reach 10 then start again from 1. This helps us stay focused on something simple like numbers instead of getting lost in worry about other things in life such as grades or relationships.
5-4-3-2-1- METHOD	Begin by naming 5 things that you can see around you; 4 things that you can touch; 3 things that you can hear; 2 things that smell; 1 thing that tastes good right now. (it could even just be water!)
BODY SCAN	Body scanning is a great way to bring awareness to your body and focus on the present moment. To do a body scan, start by lying down or sitting comfortably in a chair. Take some deep breaths in through your nose and out through your mouth until you feel relaxed.

BODY SCAN	Now begin to scan each part of your body from head to toe, paying attention to any areas of tension or discomfort. If you find any areas of tension, take a few breaths into those spots until you feel them relax. When you have scanned your entire body, take one last deep breath in before slowly opening your eyes.
PROGRESSIVE MUSCLE RELAXATION	Start by lying down or sitting comfortably in a chair with your eyes closed. Begin tensing the muscles in one area (such as your feet) for three seconds before releasing them completely for another three seconds and noticing how different it feels when they are relaxed compared to when they were tense. Continue this process working up to the top of your head before taking one final deep breath in and slowly opening your eyes.
CLOSE THE SENSES (YONI MUDRA)	The Yoni Mudra is an ancient gesture that helps us disconnect from our senses so that we can be more mindful of our present experience without being distracted by external stimuli such as noise or sight. To do this mudra, bring both hands together at chest level with palms facing outward then gently close your eyes while continuing to focus on the sensation of having both hands together at chest level until you feel settled within yourself again.
BREATH MEDITATION	Begin by focusing on your breath as it enters and leaves your body. Whenever thoughts arise (and they will!), acknowledge them without judgment and then gently bring your attention back to your breath.

COMPASSION MEDITATION	Think of someone who has done something kind for you or whom you admire greatly. Then close your eyes and focus on the feeling of deep gratitude that arises in you when thinking of this person. You can also wish them well by repeating phrases such as "May you be safe; may you be happy; may you be healthy; may you live with ease", several times during the meditation session in order to cultivate feelings of compassion towards yourself and others.
MEDITATION ON THE SKY	This type of meditation involves focusing on the sky-whether that means looking up at the night sky filled with stars or out at a beautiful sunset-as a way of connecting with nature's beauty while calming down from any stressful situations that might have arisen throughout the day.

TIPS FOR MAINTAINING MINDFULNESS IN YOUR DAILY LIFE

While choosing one of the above meditation and mindfulness techniques can be helpful, know that they aren't your only options.

There are tons of helpful apps available out there designed specifically with teens in mind. These apps often offer guided meditations as well as other helpful resources, such as tips for managing stress or creating better sleep habits.

Some particularly good ones include Headspace, Calm, and Buddhify.

You can even incorporate mindfulness into other areas you already enjoy. Coloring books specifically designed for meditation can be helpful for visual learners who enjoy art. Listening to music can be calming and soothing. Even mindful eating can help cultivate awareness of how nourishing food makes us feel. And journaling can be therapeutic these are all good places to start!

Mindfulness is best developed by making it part of your daily routine. Try to pair it with something else that you already do on a regular basis, such as going for a walk after school or right before bedtime. This way, incorporating mindfulness into your day will become second nature, and it won't seem like just another chore to add to your list.

STOP SMOKING AND DRINKING IN EXCESS

Smoking and drinking are two of the most popular activities that teens engage in, but both pose serious health risks. Smoking cigarettes can cause lung cancer, heart disease, and stroke, while excessive drinking can lead to liver damage, impaired judgment, and addiction.

If you're trying to quit smoking or drinking excessively it's important to find healthier activities or events that don't involve either of these substances.

Going out with friends who don't smoke, or drink is a great way to avoid temptation while still having fun with your peers. Participating in sports or joining a club at school are other ways to stay engaged without indulging in unhealthy habits.

If you have friends who continue to smoke cigarettes or indulge in alcohol despite your efforts to quit or cut back on those substances yourself, it might be time for you to re-evaluate those relationships. You deserve the support of friends who respect your decision not to participate in such activities anymore!

We all face peer pressure throughout our lives. It is especially prevalent during adolescence when teens are more vulnerable than ever before. If your peers are pressuring you into smoking or drinking more than you want to, remember that you always have the right to say no without feeling guilty.

GET THE HELP YOU NEED

If you have tried to quit smoking or drinking on your own and you can't seem to do it, then please book an appointment to see your doctor.

Gamechanger:
Writing down the reasons why you want to stop smoking or reduce your alcohol intake could be an effective strategy for sticking with it long term since it allows you to visualize your goal clearly.

MINIMIZING SCREEN TIME

Technology plays a major role in our daily lives, but it's important to remember that it should not take over. Staring at a screen for hours can be detrimental to your mental and physical health. Too much screen time can lead to eye strain, neck pain, poor sleep quality, increased stress levels, and more.

ESTABLISH TECH-FREE ZONES FOR YOURSELF

Setting tech-free zones in your home is one of the best ways to reduce your screen time. For example, you could designate areas in your house where no device use is allowed (such as bedrooms or dining rooms).

This will help you stay focused on activities that don't involve screens when you're in those areas. You can also set boundaries with yourself about when devices should be put away for instance, one hour before bedtime or during meals.

TRACK YOUR SCREEN TIME

If you want to know how much screen time you're getting each day, tracking it can be a great way to get an idea of what needs improvement.

Apps like Moment track the amount of time spent on each device so you can see exactly how long you've been staring at a screen throughout the day. This information can then guide your future decisions about how much screen time is necessary and where it should be minimized or eliminated altogether.

REMOVE UNNECESSARY APPS

Though slightly contradictory to the last point, another great way to reduce screen time is to delete any apps that aren't necessary for day to day life.

For example, if there are games on your phone that you find yourself spending too much time playing instead of focusing on more important tasks, delete them! This will help limit the amount of distraction available right at your fingertips so that it becomes easier to focus on something else rather than reaching for your phone whenever boredom strikes.

SWITCH TO GRAYSCALE

Switching the colors on your phone or tablet from bright colors like blue and green to grayscale (black and white) has been shown to significantly decrease usage times since it removes some of the attractiveness associated with using certain apps or websites especially social media sites like Instagram or Snapchat.

INCORPORATE MORE MOVEMENT & EXTRACURRICULAR ACTIVITIES

When you have less time spent in front of screens, it opens opportunities for physical activities like running or biking outdoors instead. If you don't feel like going outside, try yoga or stretching indoors as an alternative way to move your body and keep your muscles active.

You may also want to consider taking up an extracurricular activity such as painting or playing an instrument-anything that gets away from the digital world!

Gamechanger:
It can be difficult to step away from your screens when you're in the middle of something engaging or important. Set yourself a timer for 10 minutes breaks every hour or two so that you can remind yourself to get up and move around. This will help prevent eye strain and overall fatigue that comes with sitting in front of a screen for too long.

STAND UP MORE

Instead of sitting down in front of a computer all day long, try standing up more often! Standing up activates different muscles and helps increase blood flow throughout the body, which can help keep fatigue away while also helping with posture issues caused by prolonged sitting (and staring at screens).

GET SOME SUN!

Sunlight helps us produce Vitamin D, which is important in maintaining our body's calcium levels and healthy bones. It also improves mood and has been linked to better sleep patterns.

What is Vitamin D good for? It can help your body to retain calcium and phosphorus which are both essential for healthy bone structure. Several studies have also proved that vitamin D helps to reduce cancer cell growth and reduces infection and inflammation.

In general, scientists think five to fifteen minutes (up to thirty if you're dark-skinned) is about right to get the most out of it without causing any health risk.

But this doesn't necessarily mean you should stay outside for a set amount of time each day. Other factors come into play when determining how much sun exposure is optimal for your particular skin type and geographic location.

For example, if you're in a sunny area like Southern California or Arizona, you may not need as much time outdoors as someone who lives in a colder climate like Seattle or Minnesota.

KEEPING SAFE IN THE SUN

When it comes to the sun, protection is key! Don't overexpose yourself. Wear sunscreen and protective clothing when you're in the sun. Also, be sure to wear sunglasses to protect your eyes. Tanning beds are a big no-no. Instead of tanning, go to a dermatologist if you have concerns about your skin.

USE A LIGHT BOX IF SUN IS LIMITED

A light box emits UVB radiation similar to natural sunlight and is regulated by experts in dermatology and other health fields so that it is safe to use. If access to natural sunlight is limited due to weather or location constraints, consider investing in one of these devices as a supplement.

GO FOR A MORNING WALK

Going on a morning walk can be a great way to get some additional sunshine without having to spend hours outside every day.

OPEN THE SHADES

When indoors during the daylight hours, open up blin ds and shades whenever possible so that natural light fills rooms throughout the house.

PHYSICAL EXERCISE

Exercise is an important part of a healthy lifestyle and can help to improve your physical, mental, and emotional well being.

It does more than help you lose weight or gain muscle: it also helps with stress relief, improved moods, better sleep patterns, increased energy levels, and more.

Studies have even shown that regular exercise can reduce the risk of certain diseases like diabetes, stroke, and heart disease. And if that wasn't enough motivation exercising regularly can also help boost confidence!

Whether you're just starting out or looking to add something new to your routine, there are plenty of ways to stay active and reap the rewards that come with it. Aim for at least an hour of moderate intensity activity each day. That could mean anything from running or playing basketball to walking your dog or participating in a yoga class.

Gamechanger:
It is possible to overdo it when it comes to exercise too much activity without giving your body enough rest can result in burnout or injury. That's why it's important to mix up your routine (try different activities) and give yourself time off every once in a while, so your body can recover.

TYPES OF EXERCISE

When most people think about exercising, they think about aerobic exercises like running or biking however, there are many different types of exercise that should be incorporated into any fitness plan.

Aerobic exercises increase your cardiovascular health.

Strength training (like lifting weights) builds muscle mass.

Bone strengthening activities like jumping rope are also important they help protect against osteoporosis later in life!

> **GameChanger:**
> Exercise doesn't have to be boring. Find activities that you enjoy so that it becomes something you look forward to rather than dreading doing every day! If you don't like running, try swimming instead if traditional workouts don't appeal, try taking a dance class or joining an intramural sports team at school.

FOCUS ON YOUR EFFORT, NOT YOUR PERFORMANCE

When you first start exercising, it's easy to get discouraged if you don't see immediate results or if you feel like you're not performing at the same level as someone else.

But remember, every journey must start somewhere! The important thing is that you're trying and gradually increasing your activity levels over time.

Start by committing yourself to just 10 minutes of physical activity each day and then gradually build up from there. This will help you develop a habit of regular exercise without overdoing it or feeling overwhelmed.

TIE IT TO OTHER HOBBIES

If exercising isn't something that comes naturally for you, then try tying physical activity into something else that interests you like photography or hiking!

You could go on walks while taking pictures along the way or go exploring during hikes while also getting some cardio in at the same time! That way not only are you getting fit but also having fun while doing something else that appeals to your interests as well!

TRY THIS!

WE'VE BEEN LEARNING A LOT ABOUT HOW TO MAINTAIN GOOD HEALTH. LET'S TAKE EVERYTHING THAT WE'VE LEARNED IN THIS CHAPTER AND REFLECT.

STEP ONE: BRAINSTORM

THINK ABOUT THE DIFFERENT LIFE SKILLS MENTIONED IN THE CHAPTER. WHICH ONES DO YOU FEEL LIKE YOU NEED TO WORK ON THE MOST? WRITE DOWN ALL OF YOUR THOUGHTS AND IDEAS NO MATTER HOW SMALL OR BIG THEY ARE. THIS IS A GREAT WAY TO GET AN OVERVIEW OF WHAT NEEDS TO BE DONE.

_____
_____
_____
_____
_____
_____

STEP TWO: RATE EACH ITEM

ONCE YOU'VE BRAINSTORMED, IT'S TIME TO RATE EACH ITEM FROM EASIEST TO HARDEST TO IMPLEMENT. MAKE SURE THAT YOU ARE HONEST WITH YOURSELF ABOUT WHICH ITEMS WILL REQUIRE MORE TIME AND EFFORT THAN OTHERS THIS WILL HELP DETERMINE WHERE YOU SHOULD BE FOCUSING YOUR ATTENTION FIRST. IT'S ALSO HELPFUL TO MAKE NOTES ABOUT WHY CERTAIN ITEMS REQUIRE MORE EFFORT THAN OTHERS; THIS WILL GIVE YOU GREATER INSIGHT INTO WHAT NEEDS TO BE DONE.

_____

_____

_____

_____

_____

_____

STEP THREE: PRIORITIZE YOUR LIST

NOW THAT EACH ITEM HAS BEEN RATED, IT'S TIME TO PRIORITIZE YOUR LIST BY ASSIGNING EACH ITEM A NUMBER FROM ONE (BEING THE HIGHEST PRIORITY) HOWEVER MANY ITEMS ARE ON THE LIST (LOWEST PRIORITY). WHEN ASSIGNING NUMBERS, THINK ABOUT WHAT NEEDS IMMEDIATE ATTENTION VERSUS WHAT CAN WAIT UNTIL LATER. THIS IS ALSO WHERE THOSE NOTES COME INTO PLAY. THE MORE INFORMATION THAT CAN BE GATHERED NOW, THE BETTER!

_____

_____

_____

_____

_____

_____

STEP FOUR: Fill in the Goal Sheet Below

OK SO YOU'VE IDENTIFIED WHAT AREAS YOU'D LIKE TO CHANGE IN YOUR LIFE TO TAKE BETTER CARE OF YOUR HEALTH. GREAT JOB! YOU'VE EVEN PRIORITIZED YOUR LIST! NOW, IT'S TIME TO CREATE A PLAN TO ENSURE YOU'LL TAKE ACTION. TAKE SOME TIME TO FILL IN THE GOAL SHEET BELOW:

TOP 2 MAIN GOALS RIGHT NOW

GOAL 1: _____

TARGET DATE: _____

ACTION STEPS:
_____
_____
_____
_____

MY KEY QUALITIES:
_____
_____
_____
_____

GOAL 2: _____

TARGET DATE: _____

ACTION STEPS:
_____
_____
_____
_____

MY KEY QUALITIES:
_____
_____
_____
_____

Taking care of your body is essential for optimal physical and mental health. Regular exercise and adequate sleep are two of the most important components for good physical health while being mindful of how we communicate with ourselves, and others is key to wellness.

Ultimately, following these tips can help you build a foundation for overall health and well being. As we journey through life it's essential that self care is at the forefront: practice gratitude and set aside time to recharge with activiti es you enjoy. Remember that self-care should be an ongoing process and can look different for everyone!

One key element of good self care and taking care of your body? Eating right. In the next chapter, we'll take a closer peek at what exactly this looks like.

Chapter 6:
Eating Right

I'm sure we've all heard the adage that "you are what you eat" - but have we ever really stopped to think about what this means? Last year, I found out firsthand about the consequences of not eating properly. Here's a personal story that illustrates why it's so important to make healthy choices when it comes to food.

It all started last summer when I felt a bit burnt out from school and wanted to take a break from my usual routine. To do this, instead of cooking for myself every night like I usually do, I decided to give myself a break and order takeout three nights a week—sometimes even more! My diet consisted mostly of pizza and burgers — anything that was quick and easy.

At first, it felt great not having to worry about grocery shopping or meal prepping every week; however, after a few weeks of doing this, I started noticing some changes in my body. For one thing, energy levels dipped significantly. I found myself feeling exhausted all the time; even after sleeping for seven or eight hours each night, I couldn't seem to shake off that sluggish feeling during the day.

The worst part was how quickly my mood changed as well; by ditching healthy foods in favor of junk food, my mental health declined rapidly. After a while, it became harder and harder for me to focus on tasks or concentrate on anything for more than a few minutes at a time. It felt like my brain had just shut down—it was terrible!

Eventually, I realized that if I wanted to feel better again, something had to change—and fast! So reluctantly (I'll admit it wasn't easy!), I switched back over to cooking healthy meals at home again and tracking what I ate throughout the day.

Slowly but surely, my energy levels returned, and my mood improved almost immediately. It was amazing how much difference taking care of your body could make! Our bodies are amazing machines! They can do so many things, but one way that we must take care of our bodies is by eating the right foods.

Eating right doesn't just mean avoiding processed or unhealthy foods. It also means understanding food safety, knowing what healthy eating looks like, and being aware of your own body's needs.

When you are eating healthily, it means you are consuming a balanced diet that contains all the essential nutrients and micronutrients your body needs. Your diet should include grains, vegetables, fruits, dairy, and protein.

Each of these foods provides your body with different micronutrients and macronutrients (vitamins, minerals, carbohydrates, fats, etc.) that are essential for optimal functioning.

Include a variety of foods in your diet. This will ensure that you are getting all the necessary nutrients and micronutrients from the food you eat.

EXAMPLES OF FOODS THAT SHOULD BE INCLUDED IN A HEALTHY DIET INCLUDE:

- Whole grains such as quinoa or brown rice
- Leafy green vegetables like spinach or kale
- Fruits like apples or oranges
- Dairy products such as low-fat yogurt
- Lean proteins such as fish or chicken
- Legumes like beans or lentils, nuts and seeds
- Healthy fats from sources like avocados or olive oil

In addition to focusing on including nutritious foods in your diet, it is also important to limit certain unhealthy foods. You don't have to omit them but be mindful of your consumption.

THESE iNCLUDE:

- Processed snacks such as chips or candy
- Sugary drinks like soda or energy drinks
- Fried foods like French fries or onion rings
- Refined grains such as white bread or white pasta
- High-fat meats such as bacon or sausage
- Margarine and shortening
- Artificial sweeteners

WHAT'S BEEN ON YOUR PLATE?

As teenagers, we often don't think about what's on our plates until it's too late. Maybe it's the last-minute rush for lunch before classes or the late-night pizza orders after a long day.

Whatever it is, understanding the foods we eat and how they impact our health can help us make better decisions regarding our nutrition.

That's why we've created a nutrition survey specifically tailored to teens that can help you reflect
on what you currently eat and what you think you need to eat more of.

YESTERDAY: WHAT I ATE FOR BREAKFAST

_____

YESTERDAY: WHAT I ATE FOR LUNCH

_____

YESTERDAY: WHAT I ATE FOR SNACKS

_____

YESTERDAY: WHAT I ATE FOR DINNER

_____

TODAY: WHAT I EAT FOR BREAKFAST

_____

TODAY: WHAT I EAT FOR LUNCH

_____

TODAY: WHAT I EAT FOR SNACKS

_____

TODAY: WHAT I EAT FOR DINNER

_____

WHAT AM I DOING WELL/EATING ENOUGH OF?

_____
_____
_____

WHAT DO I NEED TO EAT MORE OF?

_____
_____
_____

3 WAYS I CAN INCORPORATE THESE CHANGES IN MY DAILY DIET

_____
_____
_____

TIPS FOR HEALTHY EATING

Essential Vitamins and Minerals

VITAMIN A	Vitamin A is essential for good vision, skin health, and a strong immune system. It helps your body fight off viruses and bacteria more quickly, making it a great vitamin to include in your diet if you're looking to stay healthy all year round. You can find Vitamin A in foods like carrots, sweet potatoes, spinach, kale, eggs, liver, and dairy products.
VITAMIN B COMPLEX	When it comes to energy production and keeping our brains sharp, B-vitamins are the real MVPs. The B-complex is a group of eight water-soluble vitamins - B1 (thiamin), B2 (riboflavin), B3 (niacin), B5 (pantothenic acid), B6 (pyridoxine), B7 (biotin), B9 (folate), and B12 (cobalamin). Together, they help our bodies convert food into fuel, support brain function, and maintain healthy skin and hair. Foods rich in B-vitamins include whole grains, lean meats, eggs, and leafy green vegetables.
VITAMIN C	Vitamin C is best known for its role in boosting immunity—it helps your body fight off infections better than without it! However it also plays an important part in helping wounds heal faster as well as increasing collagen production for healthier skin. You can get Vitamin C from citrus fruits like oranges and lemons as well as from dark leafy greens like kale and spinach.

VITAMIN D	Often called the "sunshine vitamin," vitamin D is unique because our bodies can produce it when our skin is exposed to sunlight. This fat-soluble vitamin helps our bodies absorb calcium, which is essential for strong bones and teeth. It also supports our immune system and has been linked to improved mental health. Foods containing vitamin D are limited, but some options include fatty fish like salmon, fortified dairy products, and eggs.
VITAMIN E	This is another fat-soluble antioxidant well-known for protecting our cells from oxidative damage. This powerful vitamin also supports our immune system and aids in the formation of red blood cells. In addition, vitamin E has anti-inflammatory properties and contributes to the health of our skin and eyes. Some fantastic food sources of vitamin E include nuts, seeds, and vegetable oils.

What Different Nutrients Do For Your Body

CARBOHYDRATES	Carbohydrates often get a bad rap, but the truth is they are an essential source of energy for our bodies, especially our brains. The main types are simple carbs (sugars) and complex carbs (starches and fibre). Aim for complex carbs found in whole grains, vegetables, and fruits as they provide a steady source of fuel, keeping you active and alert throughout the day!
PROTEINS	Proteins are the giant Lego pieces that make up our body's cells and tissues, including our muscles, bones, and organs. They also play a crucial role in enzyme and hormone production. So, where do you get your protein power? Lean meats, fish, dairy products, beans, and nuts are all excellent options.
FATS	Though often accused of being the primary dietary villain, not all fats are created equal. In fact, healthy fats are vital for proper brain function, hormone balance, and nutrient absorption. Opt for unsaturated fats like those found in olive oil, avocado, and nuts, while steering clear of trans fats often lurking in processed and fried foods.
VITAMINS & MINERALS	These incredible microscopic warriors help our body function efficiently and protect us from potential threats. Among their many tasks, vitamins and minerals support healthy bones, teeth, and skin, and aid in energy production. Include a variety of fruits, vegetables, grains, and lean proteins in your diet to ensure you get enough of these potent superheroes!

FIBER	Fiber is a must-have for a healthy digestive system, and it also helps keep us full and satisfied. A fiber-rich diet can assist in regulating blood sugar levels and preventing heart disease. Load your plate with whole grains, fruits, and veggies, and say hello to smooth digestion and exceptional overall health.
WATER	Water is the cornerstone of life. Our bodies are composed of roughly 60% water, which plays an essential role in nearly all bodily functions. Staying hydrated keeps our skin glowing and our energy levels soaring. Don't forget to drink up to maintain the balance!

Different Types of Diets and What They Do to Your Body

KETO DIET	The ketogenic (or "keto") diet focuses on eating high-fat foods like butter, cheese, and bacon while limiting carbohydrates. By cutting out carbs, your body is forced to break down fat instead, producing compounds called ketones which are then used as energy. This process is known as "ketosis" and it helps you burn fat quickly while preserving muscle mass. Some people find this type of diet difficult because it requires careful tracking of macronutrients (carbs, proteins, and fats), but if done correctly it can help promote weight loss and better overall health.
LOW CARB DIET	A low-carb diet is similar to a keto diet in that it restricts carb intake in order to reduce caloric intake and kick-start weight loss. The main difference between these two types of diets is that a low-carb diet allows for more variety in food choices. You still need to watch your carb intake carefully—usually no more than 20-30 grams per day—but this type of diet gives you more flexibility when it comes to what you eat. As long as you stick with lean proteins, healthy fats, and low-carb vegetables like broccoli or cauliflower, this type of diet can help promote weight loss while still allowing some indulgences here and there.
VEGETARIAN/ VEGAN DIETS	For those who don't want to give up meat entirely but still want to make healthier food choices, vegetarianism offers a great alternative. This type of lifestyle involves avoiding all animal products including eggs and dairy products: vegans go even further by eliminating honey from their diets as well as any products that have been tested on animals or contain animal products (like certain cosmetics). While these types of diets can be very healthy if done correctly—with an emphasis on plant-based proteins like tofu or tempeh—they also require careful planning in order to ensure proper nutrition levels are being met each day.

TRY TO AVOID EATING IN FRONT OF SCREENS LIKE TVS, COMPUTERS, OR PHONES.

Eating in front of a screen can also make it difficult to detect how much food you are consuming since you're focused solely on what's happening on the screen rather than what's going into your mouth.

If you eat in front of the TV, you're likely to overeat.

DRINKING WATER INSTEAD OF SUGARY DRINKS IS ESSENTIAL FOR HEALTHY HYDRATION THROUGHOUT THE DAY.

It helps flush out toxins from your body while keeping your metabolism running smoothly.
63% of adults reported drinking at least one sugary drink per day.

FAD DIETS MAY PROMISE QUICK RESULTS BUT OFTEN DO NOT PROVIDE LONG-TERM BENEFITS OR SUSTAINABLE WEIGHT LOSS.

It's best to focus on creating healthy eating habits than following quick-fix diets that may leave you feeling deprived or unsatisfied. Instead, try focusing on maintaining an overall healthy lifestyle by making small changes one step at a time!
Up to 45 Million Americans go on diet each year.

SKIPPING MEALS DOES NOT EQUATE WITH WEIGHT LOSS.

Instead, it slows down your metabolism, which can lead to weight gain later on.
Up to 27% of teens skip breakfast

TAKE TIME WHEN EATING MEALS SO THAT YOU'RE ABLE TO GIVE YOURSELF TIME TO RECOGNIZE FEELINGS OF FULLNESS.

Utilize mindful eating technique like noticing smells, texture colors, and flavors in each bit
Up to 40% of American adult report that they overea

TIPS FOR HEALTHY EATING

You'll probably have noticed that adults cook food pretty much every day. So, it's a fairly obvious life skill that you'll have to learn. Eating out every day is just not feasible for either your wallet or your body's nutritional needs. So, to make sure that you don't poison yourself or others that you'll be cooking for, we're going to talk about safe food handling while you are in the kitchen. The first and most important concept to understand is ...

CROSS-CONTAMINATION.

Cross-contamination is a serious issue when it comes to food safety. It occurs when bacteria and other contaminants are spread from one surface or food item to another. For example, if raw chicken juice gets onto a cutting board and then onto a piece of lettuce, the bacteria from the chicken can be transferred over to the lettuce. This can cause illnesses such as salmonella or E. coli if consumed by humans.

The best way to prevent cross-contamination is to keep certain foods separate while preparing meals in your kitchen. Whenever possible, use separate cutting boards for raw meat, poultry, fish, and vegetables. If you only have one cutting board available, make sure you clean it thoroughly with soap and hot water after each use before using it again for another type of food item. The same goes for any other kitchen item that comes into contact with raw meat [especially chicken].

How To Handle Produce

You should always wash fruits and vegetables before consuming them to remove any potential contaminants on their surfaces. Do this even if the package says that it has been pre-washed. The best way to wash your produce is to spray it with 3-part water and 1-part vinegar mixture. [don't worry, your produce won't taste like vinegar, I promise!].

Do not use dish soap or any other type of cleaner when cleaning your produce.

After you've cleaned your produce with water and vinegar, you'll want to visually inspect each piece and take away any damaged parts of the produce. If you notice that there are more damaged parts than good parts, you might want to toss them.

There are types of produce that has the tendency to go bad quickly or to have dirt in hidden places:

DIRT IN HIDDEN PLACES

- Brussel sprouts
- Asparagus
- Broccoli
- Cauliflower
- Potatoes
- Most fruits

GOES BAD QUICK

- Avocado
- Peppers
- Mushrooms
- Fresh herbs
- Spinach and other leafy greens
- Berries
- Tomatoes
- Peaches.
- Bananas

CHEAT SHEET

CROSS-CONTAMINATION

HOW TO HANDLE PRODUCE

Dirt in Hidden places

Goes Bad Quickly

MANAGING YOUR FRIDGE

If you don't regularly inspect your fridge and maintain its delicate climate, before too long, you'll notice a rancid smell coming from it. Here are a few tips that will help you to avoid food waste and that terrible smell:

1) Store different food groups in different sections of your fridge. Keep the meats in one area, the dairy in another, and the fruits & veggies in yet another.

2) Store a small container of baking soda in your fridge. Be sure not to use it for cooking or baking. Replace it after about a month.

3) Avoid leaving veggies in the baggies that you got from the grocery store. Veggies breathe better without them and won't go bad as quickly.

4) Rotate your foods based on the expiration date. Place the food with the latest expiration date at the back of the fridge. Foods that have gone bad can introduce harmful bacteria into other foods that come into contact with them. Be sure to check expiration dates regularly and discard any expired items immediately.

5) Be sure not to leave prepared foods out at room temperature for more than two hours; this will help reduce the chances of harmful bacteria growing on them due to the warm temperatures present in most homes during summer months or after cooking meals indoors during winter months.

SIMPLE TIPS FOR MEAL PREP

Meal prepping is a timesaving, money-saving, and healthy eating strategy anyone can use! Developing good meal prep habits now will set you up for success as an adult. It's easier than it looks and more rewarding than you might think.

So, what do we mean by meal prep? Well, it can mean one of two things:

1) Preparing ingredients that you'll need for a particular meal before you start cooking so that they are ready to use when you are ready to actively cook them [i.e., pre-salting or marinading meat.]

2) Cooking several meals at once and placing the ones that you will not eat right away in the fridge or freezer.

Meal prepping makes it easy to grab food on the go if you are running late or don't have time to cook something fresh every day. By batch-cooking your meals ahead of time, you can save yourself from having to spend hours in the kitchen every night preparing dinner.

All you need to do is heat and eat! This will save you plenty of time for studying, extracurricular activities, or just relaxing with friends.

When you are doing the work of preparing your meals, ensure that you are thinking about making them nutritious and healthy. To ensure that all essential nutrients are included in each meal throughout the week, make sure every dish includes equal parts protein (like chicken or beans), carbohydrate (such as rice or potatoes), and healthy fat (olive oil or avocado). This combination will give your body all three essential macronutrients necessary for growth and development while helping regulate hunger levels between meals.

MEAL PLANNING

Most teenagers have never had to meal plan. Either their mom does it on her own each week, and you've hardly noticed that she does, or she doesn't do it at all. Or maybe, you have a very organized mom who asks you to write in your requests for the meal planning schedule that is a permanent fixture on your fridge.

Regardless, meal planning is a science that you should master if you want to eat good food that you don't have to slave over after a hard day's work. [This is why your mom meal plans if she does.].

So, let's get started.

Meal planning is when you write on a calendar, a graph, or a blank sheet of paper what you plan on eating for each meal for the next week. Then you cook based on this plan.

HERE IS OUR GUIDE ON HOW TO MEAL PLAN LIKE A PRO:

1) Create a Plan: Start by making a list of meals that you want to make. Try selecting dishes from different cuisines so that there is variety throughout the week (e.g., Italian one night followed by Mexican another night, etc.). Be sure that you are writing out dishes that you are confident making. If you need a recipe, you can attach it to your plan.

2) Create a Calendar: Once your list is complete create a calendar where each day has its own meal plan written out (e.g., Monday - Lasagna). This will give you something concrete that can easily be referenced when grocery shopping or cooking throughout the week.

3) Do Your Grocery Shopping: Once your meal plan is complete head out on your weekly grocery trip armed with your list and only buy items related specifically to what is on it: this will help keep costs low as well as reduce waste since nothing will go bad before being used in a dish.

4) Follow Recipes: A great way for teens to start out with cooking is following simple recipes from cookbooks: there are plenty of options available geared specifically towards be-ginners such as "The Complete Cookbook For Young Chefs" from America's Test Kitchen Kids or "Cooking Class: 57 Fun Recipes Kids Will Love To Make (and Eat!)" from Deanna F. Cook & Laurie Buckleman Pomeranz. If you'd prefer to keep things digital, Pinterest and Instagram are two great social media channels for finding all kinds of new recipes, too.

5) Get Creative: Once you're comfortable enough with basic recipes, start getting creative with flavors and experimenting with different ingredients: this will help build confidence in the kitchen while also introducing new flavors into favorite dishes!

6) Enjoy Your Homecooked Meals: The last step? Enjoying all those delicious homecooked meals! Remember—cooking doesn't have to be complicated, nor does it have to take hours upon hours...try implementing these tips into your routine and see just how easy (and fun!) whipping up delicious dinners at home can truly be!

MEAL PLAN SHEET

MY MEAL PLANNER

WEEK:

	BREAKFAST	LUNCH	SNACKS	DINNER
MONDAY:				
TUESDAY:				
WEDNESDAY:				
THURSDAY:				
FRIDAY:				
SATURDAY:				
SUNDAY:				

GUIDE TO KITCHEN GEAR

Are you a teen looking to learn how to cook? Well, you're in luck! Believe it or not, cooking can be easy and fun! All you need is the right kitchen gear and know how to use it.

The first step in becoming a great home chef is making sure that you have all the necessary kitchen gear. Here are some of our top recommendations for teens just getting started with cooking:

AIR FRYERS

Air fryers are an incredibly versatile kitchen gadget that allows you to make delicious fried foods without having to use oil. Air fryers come in many sizes, so you can find one that fits your budget and space needs. With an air fryer, you can make everything from French fries and chicken tenders to pizza rolls and even cookies. It's a great way to get creative with your food while keeping things healthy.

INSTANT POTS/PRESSURE COOKERS

Pressure cookers have become increasingly popular over the past few years as they make it possible to quickly prepare meals without sacrificing flavor or nutrition. With an Instant Pot or pressure cooker, you can whip up tasty dishes like soups, stews, curries, chili, and more with minimal effort. Plus, these gadgets require very little clean-up which makes them perfect for busy teens!

CROCK POTS

If slow-cooked meals are more your speed then a crock pot may be the perfect kitchen tool for you! Crock pots allow you to set it and forget it. Ssimply add all your ingredients into the pot before leaving for school or work and come home later on to a delicious meal that's ready when you are. There are countless recipes out there for crock pot creations, so don't be afraid to get creative with yours!

GUIDE TO FAST FOOD

Fast food is often thought of as being unhealthy, but it doesn't have to be! With a little bit of knowledge and some self-control, you can still enjoy fast food without sacrificing your health.

Below, I'll cover everything you need to know about fast food, including how to find eateries that use ethical ingredients, budgeting tips for eating out frequently, and healthy ways to make the most of your fast-food experience.

LET'S DIVE IN!

The Fast-Food Questionnaire

Before you learn about what makes a fast-food joint healthy or not, fill out this little questionnaire, and at the end of the chapter, we'll see if your favorite choice is a healthy one (or if it is still your favorite when all is said and done)

WHAT'S YOUR FAVORITE FAST-FOOD PLACE?

_____

WHAT DO YOU USUALLY ORDER?

_____

HOW OFTEN DO YOU GET FOOD THERE?

_____

HOW DO YOU FEEL AFTER YOU'VE EATEN THERE?

_____

HOW HEALTHY DO YOU THINK THE FOOD IS?

_____

HAVE YOU READ ABOUT THE INGREDIENTS THAT THEY USE?

Y / N

HAVE YOU RESEARCHED WHERE THEY SOURCE THEIR INGREDIENTS?

Y / N

WHAT IS IT THAT YOU LOVE ABOUT THE FOOD
[CIRCLE ALL THAT APPLY]

THE FLAVOR:
Spicy-ness.   Sweet-ness   Salty-ness

SPEED:
It's always fast   They make it to order

INGREDIENTS
Farm-Fresh   1-5 ingredients [simple]   I have no clue

ANYTHING ELSE?

_____

_____

_____

_____

_____

WHAT TO LOOK OUT FOR

When you're hungry, it's tempting to reach for any food within arm's reach, but it's important to be mindful of what you're putting into your body. Some ingredients, including natural or unnatural flavoring, genetically modified ingredients, potassium bromate, BHT, and antibiotics, can have harmful effects on your health.

First and foremost, it's important to pay attention to the flavoring in your food. Many products will use the term "natural" flavoring to make certain ingredients sound healthy, but this can be misleading. Even "natural" flavoring can be chemically synthesized or extracted in ways that ultimately may not be healthy for you. Instead, opt for products that state the specific flavors that are included or use no synthetic flavorings at all.

Another thing to be cautious of when choosing food is genetically modified ingredients. Some common genetically modified ingredients include corn, soybeans, and canola oil. These ingredients can mess with hormones and impact the immune system in the long run. Look for foods with a Non-GMO label or research the companies you buy from to ensure their products are verified non-GMO.

Potassium bromate is a chemical often used in bread and pizza dough to help them rise. However, it's banned in several countries, including the United Kingdom and Canada, due to its link to cancer. In the United States, it's still allowed to be used, although some companies have opted for alternative rising agents. When eating bread or pizza, make sure to check if they contain potassium bromate before consuming.

BHT is a preservative commonly found in condiments, such as ketchup and mayonnaise. Ingesting large amounts of BHT is linked to cancer and negatively affects the liver and kidneys. Instead, try to find natural and organic condiments at the grocery store or make your own at home with fresh ingredients.

And while it isn't necessarily unhealthy in small doses, research has linked high levels of MSG with headaches, nausea, and other symptoms. So, if you're looking for healthier options at fastfood restaurants, keep an eye out for ones that are open about where they get their ingredients from.

Finally, it's also important to be aware of antibiotics in meat and dairy products. Animals raised for meat and dairy are often given antibiotics to prevent disease and increase growth. However, this can lead to antibiotic-resistant bacteria, which can be dangerous and difficult to treat. Look for meat and dairy products that are labeled as antibiotic-free to help reduce your risk of exposure.

DO YOUR RESEARCH

You didn't make the food, and neither did your mother. So, if you want to make sure that the ingredients that were used in making it are healthy and ethical, you're going to have to do some research.
There are a couple of ways that you can conduct your research:

1) Spend an afternoon visiting all of the websites of your favorite fast-food places and recording which restaurant uses what problematic ingredients.
2) When you are at the restaurant, ask the waiter to give you a nutrition guide for the food they serve.
3) Call the 1-800-number and ask the staff at the head office what is in their food.

There are a few certifying organizations that rate the healthy standards of restaurants in the US, too.

As the main regulatory body for food safety in the US, the FDA sets standards for food production and processing. They monitor food additives, pesticides, and other chemical residues that could harm consumers. They also inspect facilities and enforce recalls when necessary.

There are also various state and local regulatory agencies that work closely with the FDA to ensure compliance with food safety regulations.

A few other certifications to think about are:

THE NON-GMO PROJECT:

The Non-GMO Project is a non-profit organization that certifies products that do not contain genetically modified organisms (GMOs). GMOs are organisms whose genetic material has been altered in a way that does not occur naturally, most commonly found in genetically modified crops. Non-GMO Project certification assures that the product has gone through rigorous testing and meets strict requirements for GMO avoidance.

FAIR TRADE CERTIFIED:

Fair Trade Certified is another non-profit organization that certifies products, particularly in the food and farming industry. Fair Trade Certified products, from coffee to chocolate to bananas, adhere to strict environmental, social, and economic standards. These standards include fair wages for farmers, safe working conditions, and sustainable farming practices that minimize harm to the environment.

RAIN FOREST ALLIANCE:

The Rain Forest Alliance, like Fair Trade Certified, focuses on sustainable farming that protects the environment, particularly in the areas of farming, forestry, and tourism. The organization offers certification for products that meet strict environmental criteria, including water conservation and wildlife protection. It also promotes social and economic benefits for farmers and their communities, particularly by helping them to access markets for their goods.

CERTIFIED GLUTEN-FREE:

This certification, offered by the Gluten Intolerance Group, assures consumers that a product contains less than ten parts per million (ppm) of gluten, the protein found in wheat, barley, and rye that can cause damage to those with celiac disease or gluten sensitivity. Many restaurants are now offering gluten-free options, but it's important to make sure that the food is prepared with the right tools and in the right environment to avoid cross-contamination.

HEALTHY WAYS TO FAST FOOD

Eating healthy at fast-food restaurants doesn't have to be hard. Start by reading the menu carefully—some meals may seem healthier than they are once you take a closer look at them.

Many places also offer lighter options like salads or sandwiches made with whole grains instead of white bread or buns. If possible, try ordering grilled meat instead of fried meat: this will reduce your fat intake significantly without compromising taste too much!

Finally, don't forget about portion control—it's easy to go overboard when ordering from a drive-thru window, so try splitting one large meal with a friend or ordering an appetizer instead of an entrée if you're feeling extra hungry.

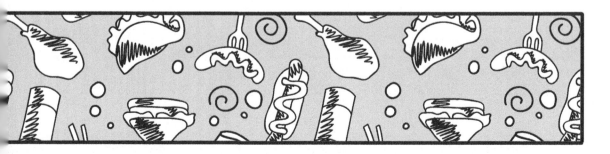

Before we move on, ask yourself a question: is your favorite fast-food place still your favorite fast-food place?

What do you think you'll do differently now that you know more about the fast-food industry?

Eating right is a crucial element of managing and maintaining your own health – but it's not the only piece to pay attention to. Even if you eat a perfect diet, issues are bound to come up every now and then. That's why it's so important to have a physician whom you regularly see to keep an eye out for any potential problems.

Remember, the best medicine is prevention. So, let's take a look next at what these visits might entail.

Chapter 7: Managing Your Health

As a teenager, taking care of your health is key to growing up strong and staying healthy. So far, your parents have likely been the ones to tell you when you needed to see a doctor and to book all of your appointments for you. But soon enough, there will be a time when you'll have to do all that yourself. It can be overwhelming trying to figure out what kind of healthcare you need and when, but it doesn't have to be complicated.

Everyone makes mistakes–it's part of the learning process. A few years ago, I made a big mistake that taught me a valuable lesson about navigating the health world. It was an experience that I will never forget.

It started when I was really sick with strep throat, and my doctor prescribed me antibiotics. Because I didn't want to pay for a full prescription, I only filled half of it and thought that would be enough. Boy, was I wrong!

Not only did my symptoms not improve, but they got worse because I didn't complete the full course of antibiotics. So, in the end, I ended up having to pay for two prescriptions—one for the original antibiotics and another for something stronger to treat my worsening symptoms.

This experience taught me a crucial lesson about navigating the health world: take your doctor's advice!

easy to think you know better than your doctor, and you might want to cut corners, but it's is never a good idea when it comes to taking care of your health. If your doctor suggests something, it's always best to follow their advice to get the best results possible.

Also, it's important to remember that other resources are available if you find yourself confused or overwhelmed by medical information. Don't be afraid to ask questions or do research on reputable websites (like WebMD) if you need more information about something related to your health. By taking advantage of these resources and trusting your doctor's advice, you can ensure that you get the best care possible without any unnecessary setbacks, as I had!

A BRIEF GUIDE TO HEALTH INSURANCE

Next up is understanding how health insurance works in the US—it might seem overwhelming at first, but it doesn't have to be! In simplest terms, health insurance is a type of insurance plan that covers some or all costs associated with medical expenses like doctor visits or hospital stays.

Health insurance is an agreement between you and an insurer that helps cover your medical expenses when something unexpected happens or if you need regular care.

Most people usually get their health insurance through their employer, but there are other options, such as purchasing private coverage or enrolling in government programs like Medicare or Medicaid. When health insurance is in place, your insurer will help pay for doctor visits, hospital stays, prescription drugs, and more, depending on the plan you choose.

Health insurance plans usually have varying levels of coverage depending on your needs. Some will cover 100%, while others may only cover 60%.

Health insurance is important because it helps protect you against high medical costs when something out of the ordinary occurs. Having coverage also allows access to preventive services such as routine check-ups and screenings at no cost, meaning that any potential problems can be caught early on before they become more severe (and expensive!).

Most plans will require a monthly premium payment plus an additional cost called a "co-pay," which is typically paid at each visit when you see your doctor or another healthcare provider.

In the US, you're covered under your parent's insurance until you're 26. Otherwise, you can purchase a health insurance plan via the Marketplace or obtain a plan through your employer if offered. Most large employers are federally required to offer some form of coverage, though requirements vary by state.

WHAT DO YOU ALREADY KNOW ABOUT YOUR PARENTS' HEALTH INSURANCE POLICY?

_____

_____

_____

WHAT QUESTIONS WOULD YOU LIKE TO ASK THEM ABOUT IT?

_____

_____

_____

_____

_____

_____

_____

_____

_____

TYPES OF DOCTORS

Specialists are doctors who focus on specific areas, such as dermatology or podiatry. They offer specialized services, such as surgeries or treatments related to their specialty area. It's no secret that understanding the healthcare system in the US can be complicated. Between all the different types of doctors, health insurance plans, and co-pays, it can be hard to keep track of everything. But don't worry! We've compiled a basic guide to help you understand the basics of doctors and health insurance so you can become an expert at navigating the healthcare system:

When it comes to medical care in the US, there are many different types of physicians. Here's a list of some common ones, along with what they specialize in:

Family Doctors: These physicians provide general care for patients from infancy through adulthood. They also diagnose and treat illnesses, perform physical exams, order blood work or other tests when needed, and refer patients to specialists if necessary.

Pediatricians: Pediatricians are specialized doctors who focus on providing care specifically for children up until age 18. They provide routine checkups and vaccinations, diagnose illnesses and injuries, manage chronic conditions such as asthma or diabetes, and coordinate referrals to other specialists.

Internists: Internists are specialists who focus exclusively on adults over 18 years old. Much like family doctors, they provide general medical care but with a more comprehensive approach due to their deeper understanding of adult medicine.

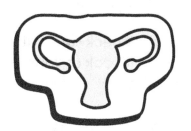

Obstetrician/Gynecologists (OB/GYNs): OB/GYNs specialize in women's reproductive health needs, such as fertility issues, pregnancy care and delivery services, menopause management, contraception counseling, and more.

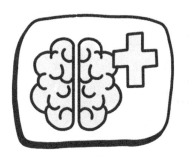

Neurologists: Neurologists specialize in diagnosing and treating disorders related to the brain and nervous system, such as Parkinson's disease or multiple sclerosis (MS).

Orthopedic Surgeons: Orthopedic surgeons specialize in diagnosing and treating Musculoskeletal conditions such as broken bones or sports injuries that require surgery.

PRIMARY CARE PHYSICIANS {PCP}

When it comes to managing your health as a teenager, it's a good idea to have both a primary care physician (PCP) and specialists on hand if necessary.

PCPs are general practitioners who act as the "quarterback" for all your healthcare needs—they refer you out for specialized care if needed and keep track of everything from routine doctor visits to test results from specialists.

ROUTINE DOCTORS VISITS

A key part of managing your health is attending regular check-ups with your physician. During these check-ups, your doctor will look at your physical development, mental health, and lifestyle habits.

They might also talk with you about nutrition, sleep habits, exercise habits, and any other general concerns that come up. It's important not to feel embarrassed or uncomfortable talking about anything during these visits—your doctor is there for you!

- PHYSICAL DEVELOPMENT
- MENTAL HEALTH
- LIFESTYLE HABITS
- NUTRITION
- SLEEP HABITS
- EXCERCISE HABITS
- GENERAL CONCERNS

MAKE SURE YOU ASK QUESTIONS.

When you are seeing your doctor, you want to make the most of each visit. Doctors' appointments are expensive and often difficult to schedule. So, before you come to your appointment write down any questions that you may have for your doctor so that you don't forget them. And while you are in the office, don't be afraid to take as long as you need to. Your health is important, and you need to have a proper understanding of what your doctor is telling you. Ask questions if something doesn't make sense—your doctor can help explain things in more detail so that you understand what's going on with your health.

HERE ARE SOME QUESTIONS THAT MAY COME UP DURING A CHECK-UP:

How Often do I need To come back?

What should I expect when I Go for my check-up?

What kind of Tests will I get?

Are there any vaccines I should Get as a teen?

SOME DOCTOR LINGO

If you've ever been to a doctor's appointment, you might have had moments where you felt like you couldn't understand what they were saying. Medical professionals use a lot of terminology that can confuse anyone who isn't in the field. To help you understand some of this lingo, we've compiled a list of common medical terms that you might encounter.

Patient: A patient is anyone who is receiving medical care. This can include people who are visiting their doctor for a regular check-up or those who are in the hospital for more serious treatment. Patients can be any age, gender, or background.

Inpatient: An inpatient is someone who is being treated in a hospital or healthcare facility and is expected to stay overnight. This can be for various reasons, such as surgery or treatment for a serious illness.

Outpatient: An outpatient is someone who is receiving medical care but is not required to stay overnight in a hospital or healthcare facility. This might include people who are receiving a vaccine or getting bloodwork done.

Chronic: Chronic refers to health conditions that are ongoing and often long-term. Examples of chronic conditions can include diabetes, arthritis, or asthma.

Acute: Acute refers to health conditions that are sudden and often severe. This might include things like a heart attack, stroke, or severe allergic reaction.

ICU: ICU stands for Intensive Care Unit. This is a specialized unit within a hospital that provides care for patients who require more intense monitoring and treatment than other patients.

Fracture: A fracture is a break or crack in a bone. This can happen due to injuries such as falls or car accidents

Sprain: A sprain is an injury to a ligament, which is the tissue that connects bones to other bones. This can happen due to twisting or overextending a joint, such as rolling an ankle.

Viral Infection: A viral infection is an illness caused by a virus. Examples of viral infections might include the flu, colds, or COVID-19.

Bacterial Infection: A bacterial infection is an illness caused by bacteria. Examples of bacterial infections might include strep throat or urinary tract infections.

Anti-biotic: An antibiotic is a medication that is used to treat bacterial infections. It works by killing or inhibiting the growth of bacteria.

Attending doctor: An attending doctor is a physician who has completed their training and is fully licensed. They are responsible for overseeing a patient's care and treatment.

Consulting doctor: A consulting doctor is a physician who has been called in to provide an opinion or recommendation regarding a patient's care. This might happen if a patient has a rare or complex condition.

Resident: A resident is a physician who is still in their training period. They work under the supervision of attending physicians and provide care to patients.

Blood pressure: Blood pressure is a measure of the force of blood pushing against the walls of your arteries. It is measured using two numbers, with the first number representing the pressure when the heart beats and the second number representing the pressure when the heart is at rest.

Hypertension: Hypertension is high blood pressure, which can be a risk factor for heart disease and stroke if left untreated.

DENTAL CARE

Keeping your teeth and mouth healthy is an important part of maintaining your overall health. While in your teenage years, your teeth are still developing. Most likely, all your permanent teeth have grown in by now, but wisdom teeth may still be coming in. While they don't need special attention, it's important to keep an eye on them and make sure they're growing correctly. Your dentist will be able to recommend any follow-up treatments needed if this isn't the case.

It's suggested that teenagers visit the dentist once every six months for a checkup or cleaning.

This is especially important if you wear braces or participate in activities like sports which can cause damage to the mouth, potentially leading to cavities or infection. Visiting the dentist regularly helps ensure that problems are caught early on before they turn into bigger issues down the line.

During these checkups, your dentist will look for cavities, signs of gum disease, worn enamel, and other oral health issues. In some cases, they may take X-rays to get a better look at what's happening inside your mouth. Your dental hygienist will also clean your teeth, removing plaque and tartar buildup that could lead to tooth decay or other issues down the road.

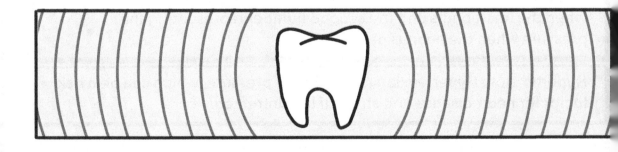

WHAT ARE DENTISTS TRYING TO PREVENT?

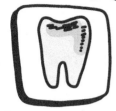

Tooth decay, also known as a cavity, leads to tooth pain in severe cases, but often, you won't have any symptoms until it's severe. Another reason why it's so important to go to the dentist!

Infection: If you experience severe pain in your tooth or jaw area, it could be due to an infectionin the root canal system of one of your teeth. In this case, you need to visit a root canal specialist known as an endodontist as soon as possible. This type of specialist is trained in diagnosing and treating diseases and injuries within the root canal system of a tooth. A root canal will help relieve pain associated with infection by removing damaged tissue from inside the tooth before sealing it with a special material called gutta-percha.

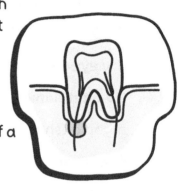

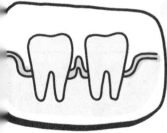

Gum Disease: Dentists don't only care for your teeth, but your gums as well. During your visit, your dentist will look over your gums to ensure that they are not receding, prone to bleeding, red or inflamed. These are all indications of a problem with your gums. If there is something that needs attention, your dentist will refer you to a periodontist or a gum specialist.

Crooked or Misaligned Teeth: If your teeth are crooked or misaligned, it might be time to see an orthodontist—a type of dental specialist who specializes in correcting misalignment issues with braces or other specialized appliances like headgear or retainers. Orthodontic treatment is typically recommended for children, but adults can also benefit from wearing braces if they have severe misalignment issues due to genetics or injury. The process usually takes several months but is worth it in terms of both appearance and long-term oral health benefits!

VISION CARE

A healthy lifestyle and regular eye exams can help prevent and treat eye problems, as well as improve vision.

There are many vision problems that you may experience at some point in life. Some of the most common are:

- dry eye syndrome
- UV light damage
- myopia (shortsightedness)
- hyperopia (farsightedness)
- astigmatism
- sports-related injuries
- digital eye strain

Gamechanger:
Eating nutrient-rich foods such as dark leafy greens, carrots, and fish can help us provide our eyes with the vitamins and minerals they need.

Regular exercise helps improve blood circulation throughout the body, including the eyes. When our blood circulates efficiently, oxygen and other necessary nutrients reach the eyes more easily, which helps keep them healthy and functioning properly. Even just 20 minutes of moderate exercise a few times a week can make a big difference in terms of eye health.

Digital devices like phones, tablets, and computers emit blue light. This has been linked to eye strain, dryness, tiredness, headaches, and even blurred vision if used for too long without taking breaks or using protective eyewear when possible.

We should aim for no more than two hours per day of digital device use unless necessary for schoolwork or other activities. When spending extended periods of time on digital devices, it's also important to remember to take regular breaks.

Eye infections are usually caused by viruses or bacteria that enter through the eye's surface - either from touching something contaminated or getting foreign matter (like dirt) into the eye. To prevent eye infections, it's important to avoid rubbing or scratching your eyes and to use clean hands when touching them.

Gamechanger:
If you wear contact lenses or eyeglasses, make sure they are cleaned properly with disinfectant solutions before putting them back on. If you do develop an eye infection or irritation, seek medical attention right away!

Make sure you get an annual comprehensive eye exam! An optometrist can detect any signs of trouble early on so they can be treated quickly: this could save you from serious issues. During these exams, you should also ask about whether any lifestyle changes could help improve your overall vision health.

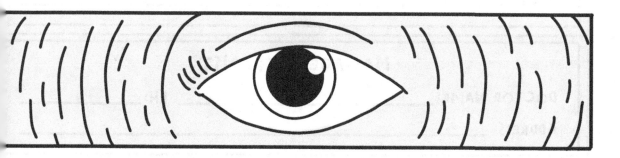

DOCTOR's INFO

PHYSICIAN

DOCTOR NAME: _____ PH: _____

ADDRESS: _____

DENTIST

DOCTOR NAME: _____ PH: _____

ADDRESS: _____

EYE DOCTOR

DOCTOR NAME: _____ PH: _____

ADDRESS: _____

CHIROPRACTOR

DOCTOR NAME: _____ PH: _____

ADDRESS: _____

MASSAGE THERAPIST

DOCTOR NAME: _____ PH: _____

ADDRESS: _____

COUNCELLOR AT SCHOOL

DOCTOR NAME: _____ PH: _____

ADDRESS: _____

REHABILITATIVE HEALTH PROFESSIONALS

So, we've learned how often we are supposed to see healthcare professionals for preventative care, but what happens if you get hurt?

Let's say you were playing soccer and there was a huge hole in the middle of the field. You didn't see it and ran right into it, causing your left foot to give out. Ouch! First, you'll likely want your parent to take you to the nearest emergency room so that a doctor can ensure it isn't broken.

But how do you rehabilitate your foot once you've received the immediate care you need? Or, how do you make it so that your foot's regular function is restored?

Your doctor will likely suggest that you make an appointment with one or more allied healthcare professionals: a registered massage therapist, physiotherapist and or chiropractor.

FIRST, WHO ARE THESE PEOPLE?

Massage Therapist- A professional health care professional that massages clients in a therapeutic way, to release muscle tension, improve circulation, and much more.

Physiotherapist - A physiotherapist, also known as a physical therapist, specializes in treating injuries, disorders, and disabilities related to muscles, tendons, and bones. Physiotherapists use various techniques and exercises to help you regain your strength, mobility, and function.

Chiropractor- Chiropractors use to various techniques to manipulate and adjust the spine to help improve joint mobility, reduce pain, and promote overall wellness.

relieving sports injuries to addressing underlying causes of symptoms, massage therapy, and chiropractic care are great options for anyone looking for a more natural form of wellness.

Massage therapy and chiropractic care can help address some of the underlying causes of muscle pain by providing relief from those aches and pains that may be caused by bad habits or improper posture correction. Both professionals aim to get at the root cause of any issues you may be having instead of just treating the symptoms - this way, you get long-lasting relief instead of temporary fixes, which only mask the problem until it resurfaces again later down the road.

Through targeted treatments like spinal manipulation or deep tissue massage, practitioners can get to the source of your discomfort so you can start feeling better sooner rather than later!

SPORTS INJURIES

Sports injuries are a common occurrence among athletes, especially ones who participate in contact sports like football or soccer. Muscles may become strained due to overuse or through contact with another player's body part; resulting in soreness or even swelling in the area. Fortunately, with massage therapy and chiropractic care, athletes can receive treatment that reduces inflammation, realigns muscles and joints back into their proper positions, and helps repair any damaged tissue so they can return to playing soon after the injury occurs.

And sometimes our bodies will tell us something isn't quite right, even if we don't know what it is yet. Has that ever happened to you?

Take some time today to reflect on these tips and think about how they could fit into your day-to-day life. What kind of changes do you want to make? How are you going to make sure these changes happen? Make a plan for yourself - write down what steps you need to take in order to reach your goals! Then take action - start by eating healthier meals and scheduling time in your week for exercise.

REFLECTION QUESTIONS:

WHAT CHANGES DO I WANT TO MAKE RELATED TO MY PHYSICAL HEALTH?

_____
_____
_____
_____

HOW AM I GOING TO ENSURE THAT I STICK WITH MY PLAN?

_____
_____
_____
_____

WHAT ARE SOME ACTIVITIES I ENJOY DOING THAT COULD FIT INTO MY ROUTINE?

_____
_____
_____
_____

Healthy living doesn't have to be hard! Once your physical health is in good shape, the rest of the pieces will naturally follow.

Next up, we'll take a closer look at how to make better decisions, both in regards to your physical health and other aspects of your life.

Chapter 8: Making Good Decisions

As a teenager, making decisions can make you feel like the whole world is on your shoulders.

From choosing which classes to take in school to deciding what kind of job you want to have after college, there are plenty of choices that need to be made.

That's why it's important to develop problem-solving skills early.

Before we get started, take a look at the following list of questions to ask yourself about whether you might be making good decisions on a day-to-day basis:

What are my values?

What are the pros and cons of this decision?

What short- and long-term implications will this decision have?

What would I say to a friend trying to make this decision?

How will this decision help me achieve my long-term goals?

METHODS FOR PROBLEM-SOLVING

Here are some steps to follow to help you solve any kind of problem.

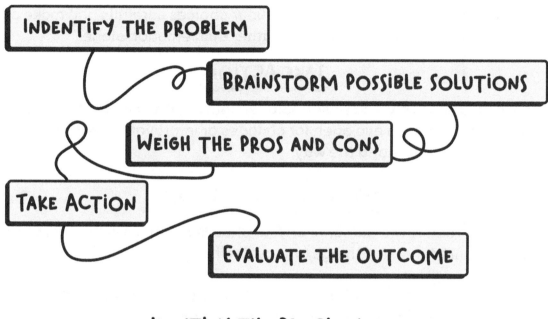

IDENTIFY THE PROBLEM

The first step in any problem-solving process is identifying the issue at hand and why it's a problem in the first place.

BRAINSTORM POSSIBLE SOLUTIONS

Once you have identified the problem, the next step is to brainstorm possible solutions.

Once potential solutions are identified, evaluate each option carefully and rule out those that may not be viable due to time constraints or other factors. Consider any long-term consequences associated with each solution - such as whether it could potentially lead to further complications down the line - before ruling out any options completely.

WEIGH THE PROS AND CONS

After ruling out poor options, consider the pros and cons of all remaining options before making a final decision.

This step is especially important for big decisions like choosing a major in college or applying for jobs after graduation. Looking at both sides of a situation helps you think through your choices carefully and make an informed decision based on logic rather than emotion alone.

TAKE ACTION

Next, you can put your chosen solution into action immediately. At the same time, keep an eye open for changes or improvements that may need to be made along the way.

EVALUATE THE OUTCOME

Always evaluate the outcome of your chosen solution once it has been implemented - even if things turn out well!

Evaluating outcomes helps you learn from past experiences while giving you insight into what works (and what doesn't). If necessary, you can adjust your approach accordingly later on.

METHODS FOR DECISION MAKING

As a teenager, you're constantly making decisions that shape your life and future from what college to attend to which job offer to accept. Every single decision carries a weight to it. How do you make sure you're making the right decisions?

Decision-making isn't necessarily the same as problem-solving - you have plenty of "non-problematic" decisions to make, after all.

There are five key methods of decision-making to pay attention to as a teen.

Command Style Decision Making

In a command-style decision-making process, only one person is responsible for making the final call. This is often seen in military settings with an officer giving orders or in a corporate setting with an executive making the ultimate choice. While this style can be effective in certain circumstances, it should not be used as a go-to decision-making method for groups.

Consult Style Decision Making

Consult style decision-making involves consulting with others before making a final call. It allows individuals to provide input and ideas without taking ownership of the entire process or outcome. This style works best when multiple stakeholders need to feel heard before any decisions are made or enacted.

Vote Style Decision Making

Vote style decision-making is often used by organizations that have large groups of people who need to agree on something before it can move forward. Every member has an equal vote, and the majority rules, regardless of whether everyone agrees with the majority opinion. This type of decision-making works best when time is limited and there's no room for compromise between seemingly opposing sides.

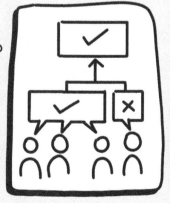

Consensus Style Decision Making

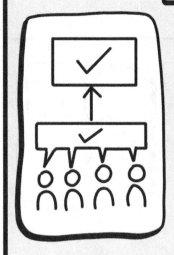

Consensus style decision-making requires all members involved come together and agree on a solution before any action is taken. Everyone's opinion matters equally, so no one person's views get precedence over another's. Rather, the group works together until they are all in agreement about what should happen next. This type of collective decision-making works best when everyone affected by the outcome has ownership over it moving forward since they had a part in creating it from start to finish.

With these key types of decision-making methods in mind, you can choose the one that works the best for the type of decision you need to make. Then, follow the step by step guide on the next page.

IDENTIFY THE DECISION

The first step in making a decision is to clearly define the decision that needs to be made. Are you deciding which college to enroll in, choosing a career path, or contemplating whether to join a sports team?

Clearly identifying the decision at hand will help you focus on the relevant factors and enable you to proceed confidently.

GATHER ANY NECESSARY AND RELEVANT INFORMATION

Once you've identified the decision, it's time to do your due diligence by collecting all the necessary and relevant information. This can be accomplished through research, discussing your options with trusted friends, family members, or mentors, or even engaging in self-reflection.

> **Gamechanger:**
> Make sure you gather information from multiple sources and don't limit yourself to only one perspective.

IDENTIFY ALTERNATIVES

Once you've gathered sufficient information, it's time to brainstorm and identify the various alternatives available to you. Analyze each option, listing their pros and cons. Make sure to be realistic about the possibilities and don't fall into the trap of being overly idealistic.

WEIGH THE EVIDENCE

Next comes the process of weighing the evidence to determine the best course of action. Referring back to the pros and cons list you've created for each alternative, consider the overall impact each option will have on your life.

Think about the short and long-term consequences, as well as how each choice aligns with your values, priorities, and goals.

Choose Among Alternatives

After thoroughly weighing the evidence, it's time to choose the alternative that best aligns with your priorities, values, and goals in life. Trust your intuition and be honest with yourself about your decision.

Take Action

Having made your decision, it's time to put it into action. Create a plan outlining the steps required to implement your decision and define a timeline for completing each step.

Acting is often the most challenging part of the process but remember that every small step adds up to significant progress.

Review the Decision & its Consequences

After taking action, it's essential to review your decision and its consequences. Reflect on the impact your choice has had on your life and the lives of those around you: evaluating whether your decision has led to the desired outcome or not.

This assessment will help you learn and grow from your experiences, which will ultimately improve your decision-making skills in the future.

MY INTELLIGENCE SURPRISES EVEN ME!

CREATING SMART(ER) GOALS

Have you ever set a goal for yourself, only to find that it falls by the wayside after the initial excitement fades? Or perhaps you've accomplished a goal but struggled to measure your progress and truly feel a sense of satisfaction.

If this sounds like you, then it's time to learn about a goal-setting strategy that can transform your dreams into achievable milestones: SMART(ER) goals.

In this next section, I'll provide an overview of SMART principles, the application of these principles in designing your goals, and some alternative goal-setting strategies to suit individual preferences.

So, buckle up, and let's dive in!

WHAT ARE SMART GOALS?

SMART is an acronym used to describe goals that are Specific, Measurable, Actionable, Realistic, and Timed. By incorporating these elements, you can craft goals that are clear, achievable, and trackable.

SMARTER further expands on this by adding Evaluated and Reviewed to the mix, ensuring continuous improvement and adapting to changing circumstances.

The SMART(ER) framework is recommended to enhance your goal-setting process, increasing your chances of success through creating meaningful, well-defined targets.

The importance of setting SMART goals cannot be overstated. As a teenager keen on honing essential life skills and maximizing personal growth, SMART goals allow you to:

Clarify and define your objectives in a way that promotes a sense of direction and motivation.

Set reasonable expectations, avoiding the common pitfall of setting unrealistic targets.

Measure your progress and celebrate small wins, boosting self-esteem and reinforcing your sense of achievement.

Develop discipline, time management, and other valuable skills that will pave the way for success in adulthood.

As teenagers, we often set goals for ourselves to become successful. But it's easy to get overwhelmed by the goals we have in mind and not know how to achieve them. That's where SMARTER goals come in! They are an easy way to ensure that your goals are clear, achievable, and motivating.

Let me tell you a story about how setting a SMARTER goal changed my life for the better.

It all started when I decided I wanted to get into college—a seemingly impossible goal. After talking with my parents and mentors, they suggested I make a SMARTER goal out of it.

That's when I realized that I had been setting myself up for failure because my goal was too vague and overwhelming; there was no structure or timeline associated with it. So instead, I made my goal "I will get accepted into college by April 1 , 2021". This new SMARTER goal allowed me to develop tangible steps that would take me closer to achieving this milestone.

The first step was researching different colleges and universities that offered what I was looking for in terms of academics, student life, and cost of attendance.

Once I had narrowed down my list of schools, the next step was preparing for any admissions tests I needed to take (SAT/ACT) as well as writing essays required by the colleges on my list. From there, it was just a matter of following through on each step until April 1st arrived—and sure enough, I got accepted!

By making a SMARTER goal out of something seemingly impossible, I was able to break it down into achievable steps that led me closer to success.

To make sure your goals are clear and achievable like mine were, remember the acronym "SMARTER": Specific; Measurable; Achievable; Realistic; Timely; Evaluate & Re-evaluate; Re-wards-based.

HOW TO CREATE SMARTER GOALS

Now that you understand the importance of SMART(ER) goals, let's break down each element and learn how to craft them effectively:

- **Specific**: Clearly define your goal by answering the essential questions of who, what, where, when, and why. Vague goals can lead to a loss of motivation, so be as specific as possible.

- **Measurable**: Set milestones, targets, or other quantifiable factors to help you assess progress and know when your goal has been achieved.

- **Actionable**: Identify actions you can take to achieve your goal, ensuring each step is feasible and within your control.

- **Realistic**: Analyze your resources, abilities, and constraints, and set goals that challenge you without being unattainable.

- **Timed**: Establish a deadline for your goal, creating a sense of urgency and promoting effective time management.

- **Evaluated**: Periodically assess your progress, keeping track of your accomplishments and areas that may require adjustment.

- **Reviewed**: Reflect upon the process and results, taking note of what worked well and what didn't, and make changes accordingly for future goal-setting ventures.

PROS AND CONS OF SMARTER GOALS

While SMARTER goals offer numerous benefits, such as clarity, manageability, and accountability, there are potential drawbacks as well. An overemphasis on SMARTER goals may lead you to be detail-oriented, losing sight of the big picture of personal growth.

Furthermore, the relying on measurable factors can limit your ability to set and pursue more abstract goals or values.

Despite these drawbacks, the SMART(ER) framework remains an invaluable tool in your goalsetting arsenal, making it worth exploring and adapting to your needs.

SMART GOALS WORKSHEEEET

Name:

Date:

S SPECIFIC (DESCRIBE YOUR GOAL)

M MEASURABLE (HOW CAN YOU TRACK PROGRESS?)

A ACHIEVABLE (IS THIS POSSIBLE? HOW?)

R RELEVANT (DOES THIS GOAL ALIGN WITH THE BIGGER PICTURE?)

T TIMELY (WHAT IS THE DEADLINE?)

OTHER GOAL-SETTING STRATEGIES TO TRY

If you find SMART(ER) goals are not suitable for every aspect of your life, consider trying out different goal-setting strategies like:

▷ **Vision Boards**: Visually represent your goals and aspirations to keep them front and center in your mind.

▷ **Action Plans**: A step-by-step outline of actions needed to accomplish a goal, allowing you to focus on one step at a time.

▷ **Accountability Partners**: Enlist a friend or family member to support you and hold you accountable for your goals.

In the next section, we'll cover key pieces of information you need to know to take care of your home, from cooking to cleaning and everything in between.

Intrigued? Keep reading!

PART 2

Taking Care of Your Home

When I was in high school, I had a huge wake-up call when it came to taking care of my home. My parents were both working hard and didn't have the time to keep up with all the little things around the house.

So, one day I decided to take it upon myself to start tidying up, and it was the best thing I ever did. Not only did it make our home look better, but it also made me feel better about myself. There are so many benefits to taking care of your home that you may not even realize!

Taking care of your home is more than just cleaning up messes. It's about properly maintaining your home for long-term value and comfort. Here are some reasons why you should prioritize proper maintenance:

PREVENT SERIOUS ISSUES

By regularly inspecting your home for potential issues and addressing them right away, you can help prevent small problems from turning into expensive repairs down the road. This includes everything from checking for water damage in places like attics or basements, making sure appliances are functioning correctly, and looking out for signs of pest infestations.

INCREASE HOME VALUE:

Regular maintenance helps ensure that your home maintains its value over time, which will come in handy if you ever decide to sell or rent it out one day. Investing in regular upkeep will pay off in the future!

ENHANCE COMFORT & SAFETY:

A well-maintained home offers improved comfort and safety for those living inside it—especially important if you have young children or elderly family members living with you. Cleaning often helps reduce air pollutants like dust mites and mold spores that can be harmful for people with allergies or asthma. It also helps reduce pests like rodents and bugs that can bring disease into your home (and nobody wants that!).

Chapter 9:
Cooking: The Fun Way

Cooking is often seen as a chore, but it doesn't have to be! With some creativity and determination, cooking can be an enjoyable activity that opens a world of possibilities. To prove it, here's a story.

When I was in high school, I was always on the lookout for ways to make money. After seeing all the ads for online tutoring services, I decided to give it a try. It wasn't easy at first; my students weren't very interested in what I had to say, and progress was slow. Then one day, after trying something new—cooking classes—I finally found success!

The key was to make cooking fun and interactive. Instead of just lecturing about the basics of food preparation and nutrition, I tried to engage my students with hands-on activities that made cooking feel like an adventure instead of a chore.

We explored different recipes from around the world, experimented with ingredients and techniques, and even tasted our creations together! My student's enthusiasm skyrocketed as they discovered how much fun they could have while learning how to cook.

In no time at all, word spread about my cooking classes, and soon enough, I was teaching more people than ever before! They were excited about learning how to cook because now it felt like something accessible instead of daunting—they realized that anyone could learn how to make delicious meals with just a little bit of knowledge and practice.

Plus, the satisfaction that comes from seeing your hard work pay off when you sit down for dinner is unbeatable!

You don't have to take cooking classes to be successful. Instead, you just need to be patient with yourself and take the time to learn the basics. Let's take a closer look!

BASIC COOKING TIPS

If you've ever wanted to become a better cook but weren't sure where to start, we have just the thing for you! Here are some basic cooking tips to be aware of.

LEARN HOW TO READ A RECIPE

The first step in becoming a better cook is learning how to read recipes correctly. A lot of helpful information can be found in each recipe, such as the ingredients needed, cooking instructions, and even nutrition information. Paying attention to this information can make all the difference between making something delicious and making something... less than edible!

WHAT INTIMIDATES YOU MOST ABOUT COOKING? WRITE IT DOWN ON THE LINES BELOW:

_____
_____
_____
_____
_____
_____

HOW TO CHOOSE THE RIGHT RECIPES

Once you know how to read recipes, it's time to choose which ones you want to try. Consider your skill level and available ingredients before picking out your recipes. It might be tempting to jump right into an advanced recipe but starting off with something simpler is probably wiser.

LOOK AT PREP TIME AND COOK TIME

Recipes will usually tell you both prep time and cook time, so take this into account when planning your meals. Many people make the mistake of looking only at the cook time and not considering that some meals require additional prep work beforehand (chopping vegetables, marinating meat, etc.). Make sure to plan accordingly!

TASTE TEST AS YOU COOK

Recipes will usually tell you both prep time and cook time, so take this into account when planning your meals. Many people make the mistake of looking only at the cook time and not considering that some meals require additional prep work beforehand (chopping vegetables, marinating meat, etc.). Make sure to plan accordingly!

NOT ALL ALTERNATIVES ARE CREATED EQUAL... BUT SOME ARE!

When substituting ingredients, it's important to remember that not all alternatives are created equal. For example, replacing butter with margarine won't always deliver the same results so pay attention when switching things up too much. But don't worry - some alternatives do work really well so don't be afraid to experiment!

Gamechanger:
Not sure if a certain substitution will work? There's an app for that! One of the most popular is Substitutions, an app for iOS devices that has a collection of more than 1000 different cooking and baking substitutions you can make.

PAY ATTENTION TO SERVING SIZES

Serving sizes matter because they let us know how much food we should eat per meal. This can be especially important when portion control is necessary for health reasons or weight loss goals.

Here's some information on suggested servings from each food group, courtesy of the American Heart Association.

PAY ATTENTION TO COOKING TECHNIQUES

Different techniques produce different results so it's important to pay attention when cooking with new methods (baking versus roasting versus frying). Paying attention while trying out new techniques will help ensure your dishes turn out just right every single time.

MAKE A SHOPPING LIST

Before you head to the grocery store, make sure you have a shopping list of all the ingredients and tools you'll need for your recipes.

This will help save time and prevent any impulse buys. Refer to the recipes beforehand so that you can double check what ingredients are necessary versus what is simply recommended. It saves money in the long run!

BELOW IS A TEMPLATE YOU CAN USE TO MAKE YOUR SHOPPING LIST:

CANNED GOODS	
MEAT/FISH	
DAIRY	
VEGETABLES	
FRUITS	
DRY GOODS (PASTA, CEREAL,ETC)	
BAKERY ITEMS	
FROZEN FOODS	
PERSONAL CARE ITEMS	
CLEANING SUPPLIES	

USING MEASURING CUPS AND SPOONS

Measuring cups and spoons are essential kitchen tools when cooking. Investing in a good set will ensure accuracy. Plus, it makes measuring much easier! When measuring dry ingredients like flour or sugar, spoon into the cup until overflowing then scrape off the excess with a flat edge (like an un-serrated knife).

For wet ingredients such as oil or water, use liquid measuring cups which have lines along the side indicating measurements. Fill up to that line corresponding to your measurement amount. The most common way to measure ingredients is by using a measuring cup or spoon set. These sets will usually contain:

- teaspoons (tsp)
- tablespoons (tbsp)
- 1/4 cups (1/4 c.)
- 1/3 cups (1/3 c.)
- 1/2 cups (1/2 c.)
- 1 cup (1 c.)
- 2 cups (2 c.)
- 4 cups (4 c.)

Sometimes you'll need to convert from one measurement unit to another: this is where a conversion chart comes in handy. Here are some common conversions for dry ingredients like flour, sugar, baking powder, etc.,:

CONVERSION CHART FOR COMMON DRY/WET MEASUREMENTS

3 teaspoons	1 tbsp	1/2 oz	14 grams
2 tbsp	1/8 cup	1 oz	28 grams
4 tbsp	1/4 cup	2 oz	56 grams
x	1/2 cup	4 oz	112 grams
x	3/4 cup	6 oz	168 grams
x	1 cup	8 oz	224 grams
3 tsp	1 tbsp	1/2 fl oz	14 ml
2 tbsp	1/8 cup	1 fl oz	28 ml
x	3/4 cup	6 fl oz	1689 ml
x	1 cup	8 fl oz	224 ml

"MISE EN PLACE"

TRANSLATION:
HAVE EVERYTHING SET UP AND READY TO GO BEFORE YOU START COOKING

This tip is often referred to as **"mise en place"** by professional chefs, but don't let that intimidate you! It simply means having all of your ingredients prepped and ready before you begin cooking.

This includes washing vegetables, measuring out ingredients, chopping herbs, etc. So, when it comes time to actually start cooking, everything is ready and all you have to do is put it all together. Trust us - this will save you a lot of time (and stress!) in the long run.

DEVELOPING YOUR KNIFE SKILLS

Good knife skills can make all the difference when it comes to cooking. Start by investing in high quality knives - preferably ones made from stainless steel - and then practice proper techniques like holding them correctly and keeping them sharpened.

Make sure you understand how each knife works best for certain tasks such as slicing vegetables or carving meat so that you can utilize them better when cooking.

Tip: What are the most essential knife skills to master? How to grip the knife, dice, chop, mince, chiffonade, and julienne. You can learn more by scanning the QR code:

SCAN ME

Become Familiar With The Stovetop

The stovetop is one of the most versatile kitchen appliances out there. It also has many dangers associated with its use if not used properly. Make sure to familiarize yourself with your gas/electric stove so that safety measures like turning off burners after use become second nature.

You should also learn about different burners settings (high heat versus low heat) so that you can cook food evenly without burning it. Knowing these details ensures that your experience using the stovetop will be smooth!

Know How To Cut and Double Recipes

Learning how to cut recipes in half or double them is an essential skill for any home cook. This way, you can make just enough food for one person or a whole group without wasting any ingredients.

And what if a recipe calls for too few or too many ingredients for what you need?

No problem – just adjust the measurements accordingly. Once you get the hang of it, this skill will serve you well in the future.

Don't Be Afraid of The Oven, Broiler, and Other Appliances

Ovens may seem intimidating at first glance, but they are actually pretty simple once you get used to them! The same goes for other appliances like your stovetop or broiler. They're really not that scary once you know how they work. And with practice comes confidence - soon enough, using these appliances will become second nature!

PRACTICE GOOD SANITATION

Food safety is important - no matter what type of food you are preparing. It's essential that your workspace is clean before starting (wash your hands!), while working (make sure raw meat doesn't come into contact with anything else), and after finishing (clean your cutting board!).

Doing this will help ensure that no one gets sick from eating whatever delicious dish you made!

CLEAN UP AS YOU GO

Cleaning up as you go makes the entire cooking process much easier because there's less mess at the end! Plus, it helps keep things organized so everything looks neat and tidy when dinner service starts. Take a few minutes after each step in your recipe preparation to clean up your workspace – trust us, it'll be worth it in the end.

COOKING TERMINOLOGY

There are dozens of terms used in cooking that can be confusing for beginners. But once you learn them, they will become second nature. Here are some of the most popular cooking terms and their explanations:

AL DENTE	Italian expression meaning "to the tooth" referring to properly cooked pasta or vegetables that still have a slight bite when bitten into.
BAKE	To cook food in an oven using dry heat.
BEAT	To mix ingredients together quickly with a spoon or mixer to make them smooth and combined.
BROIL	To cook food directly under or above high heat.
CREAM	To mix two ingredients together until they form a thick paste-like consistency, usually done with butter and sugar.
FILLET	To cut away boneless pieces of meat from bones or larger pieces of fish or chicken.
FRY	To cook food by immersing it in oil or fat and heating it at a high temperature until it is golden and crisp.
GRILL	To cook food over direct heat on a hot surface such as a griddle pan, BBQ grill, open fire, etc.

MARINADE	A liquid mixture made up of herbs, spices, oil, vinegar, citrus juice, and other liquids used to add flavor and tenderize meats before cooking.
PICKLE	The process of preserving foods such as cucumbers in vinegar or brine solution for an extended period of time (usually several weeks) before eating them.
SAUTE	A French cooking technique where small pieces of food are cooked quickly over high heat using butter or oil for added flavor.
STEAM	A process of cooking food by exposing it to steam from boiling water below until it becomes soft enough to eat.
BASTE	To brush melted butter, juices, or other liquids onto meats while they are cooking in order to keep them moist.
BLANCH	The process of briefly boiling vegetables before plunging them into cold water to stop their cooking process, which preserves their texture and color.
BRAISE	A method of slowly simmering meats over low heat after searing them first, which helps break down tough connective tissues making them tender and juicy.
BRINE	The process of soaking foods like poultry, seafood, vegetables, cheeses etc., in salty water overnight before cooking them.
DRESS	The technique used for combining ingredients like salad greens with dressings like vinaigrettes.

JULIENNE	A precise cutting technique where vegetables are cut into thin strips resembling matchsticks.
PARBOIL	A partial boiling method used mainly for tougher cuts of meat which involves submerging the meat into boiling water briefly before completing its cooking through another method such as roasting.
RENDER	To slowly melt down fatty cuts of meat (like bacon) over low heat so that fat is released leaving behind delicious cracklings that can be used as toppings on dishes like salads.
SEAR	The process of quickly browning the surface areas of meats over high heat prior to slow cooking them using other methods such as baking.
STEEP	Like brewing tea wherein herbs, fruits etc., are soaked in hot liquid until all flavor is extracted from it.
ZEST	Small amounts shaved off citrus fruits like lemons, limes etc., containing oils packed with intense flavors which can be used for baking desserts, among many other uses.

SAFE FOOD PRESERVATION

Learning how to properly store and preserve food is an important life skill — especially if you want to maintain a healthy diet and save some money by buying in bulk. Check out these tips for everything you need to know about safely storing and preserving food!

REFRIGERATE OR FREEZE PERISHABLES ASAP

If it says, "refrigerate after opening" or "keep refrigerated," then be sure to put it in the fridge right away. The same goes for freezing perishables — get them into the freezer as soon as possible. This will help maintain their freshness and prevent bacteria from growing on them quickly.

KEEP APPLIANCES AT THE RIGHT TEMPERATURES

Your fridge should be kept at 40°F (4°C) or below, while your freezer should remain at 0°F (-18°C). Applying this tip will ensure that perishable foods are stored properly and that they stay fresh longer. Keep an eye out for any appliance malfunctions so that you can alert your parents-it could save a lot of money in spoiled food!

CHECK STORAGE DIRECTIONS ON FOOD LABELS

Be sure to check the labels of all foods before purchasing them. Some items may need special storage instructions such as keeping in a cool, dry place away from direct sunlight or heat sources. Not following these directions can reduce the shelf life of certain foods drastically, so pay attention!

REMEMBER....

FOOD CAN BE SPOILED AND
MAKE YOU SICK EVEN IF IT DOESN'T LOOK THAT WAY

Bacteria can be invisible to the naked eye so even if something looks perfectly fine, there is still a chance that it has gone bad. To avoid eating contaminated food, always check expiration dates before purchasing and consuming something — even if it looks totally fine!

> **Gamechanger:**
> This tip also applies to leftovers, too. Reheat leftovers thoroughly and toss them if they've been in the fridge for more than a couple of days.

MARINATE FOOD ONLY IN THE FRIDGE

Marinating meat is a great way to add flavor but make sure to do so only in the refrigerator —not on the countertop or outdoors. This will help prevent bacterial growth on the raw meat which could lead to serious illness if consumed without proper cooking first.

CLEAN THE FRIDGE REGULARLY

Keep your fridge clean by wiping down shelves regularly with warm water and mild detergent solution. Doing this will reduce buildup of nasty odors (and bacteria!) which can taint other foods stored inside it. It's also helpful to use airtight containers or bags when storing leftovers as this way less likely to allow smells from one item affect another one nearby.

KEEP FOODS COVERED

This may seem like a no-brainer, but it is important to keep all foods covered when not in use. Not only will this help keep critters out of your food, but it also helps keep bacteria away from foods that don't have preservatives. Covering foods will also keep them fresher longer, saving you time and money in the long run.

CHECK EXPIRATION DATES

Another obvious tip, but expiration dates are there for a reason! Consuming expired foods can make you seriously ill. It's best to check labels before cooking or eating anything and pay close attention to any warnings on the label.

> **Gamechanger:**
> Use by dates don't necessarily indicate a food's safety - just its freshness. Often, foods are safe to eat beyond the expiration date, so look at other indicators (like smell, appearance, etc.) to determine its safety. The only exception is baby formula, which must be used by the use-by date. The same applies to sell by dates in most cases.

FREEZER BURN DOESN'T MAKE FOOD UNSAFE

Freezer burn is not a sign that food has gone bad — rather, it means that moisture has been removed from the food by harsh cold temperatures in the freezer.

The good news is that you can safely cut off any affected areas and still eat the rest of the meal or snack without worry! Just make sure you consume it soon after thawing as freezer burn can lead to texture changes in some foods over time.

Be Careful Thawing Foods (Do So in the Fridge)

To avoid bacteria buildup while thawing frozen foods such as meats and vegetables, always do so in your fridge overnight. Thawing at room temperature can cause bacteria growth which may make you sick if consumed later!

> **Gamechanger:**
> Thawing food in the fridge is, again, your best bet. If you must thaw more quickly, do so in a pan of cold water (never lukewarm or hot).

Check Canned Goods for Damages

Check canned goods before purchasing them as any visible damages could signal spoilage or bacteria buildup inside the container. If you find damaged cans on your shelves at home, discard them immediately — they are not safe to eat!

TYPES OF FOOD

When I was a teenager, I used to think that cooking was just about following recipes. Sure, I could make some good food, but nothing that made me stand out from the crowd. Little did I know that there was a whole world of flavor combinations waiting for me to explore!

By understanding the different types of flavors and how they interact with each other, I learned how to make my own delicious creations in the kitchen.

SALTY

Salt is one of the most used ingredients in cooking and it enhances flavors by bringing out more of their natural sweetness or bitterness. The right amount of salt can bring balance and depth to dishes. When using salt, it is important to start small and gradually add more until you reach your desired level of flavor.

SWEET

Sweetness can be added through desserts or savory dishes alike, such as adding fresh fruit or honey to salad dressings. Sweetness can also come from other ingredients like onions or garlic when cooked down slowly over low heat until they caramelize. Sweetness can help balance out salty flavors, which can help take a dish from blasé to scrumptious!

SOUR

Sour flavors are often used in combination with sweet flavors to create an exciting contrast between the two tastes. They are also great for adding brightness and vibrancy to dishes: think pickled vegetables or citrus fruits like lemons and limes! Be sure not to overdo it though—too much sourness will ruin a dish's flavor profile.

BITTER

Bitter flavors are usually associated with coffee and dark chocolate, but there are plenty of other sources too! Think dandelion greens, kale, endive, radicchio and even some types of fruits like grapefruits or pomegranates. Bitterness adds complexity and depth without overpowering other flavors in the dish.

UMAMI

Umami is described as a "meaty" flavor that comes from ingredients like mushrooms, tomatoes, and soy sauce. It is often used as an umami-rich base for soups and stews because it adds savory depth without being overly salty or sweet. In addition to adding richness to dishes, umami also helps enhance other flavors like garlic or onion when combined correctly!

SAVORY

Savory flavors come from herbs such as rosemary, thyme, or oregano as well as spices like cumin or coriander seed powder. These give dishes an earthy warmth that makes them feel comforting yet complex all at once!

Savory notes work particularly well with fatty meats such as pork belly or beef short ribs since they help cut through the richness while simultaneously boosting its flavor profile even further.

A GUIDE TO OILS AND HOW TO USE THEM

Learning how to cook with different types of oil is one such skill that can make a huge difference in the kitchen. Without knowing this information, you can easily ruin any dish you attempt—no matter how simple!

One of the biggest reasons for knowing the differences between oils is flavor. Every type of oil has its own flavor profile and understanding which type of oil will impart which flavor is essential for creating dishes that will satisfy your taste buds.

For instance, olive oil has a distinctively nutty taste that pairs well with salads or other light dishes, while coconut oil has a sweetness that works best when used in baking or desserts.

Another important factor when cooking with oils is smoke point. The smoke point (or burning point) is the temperature at which an oil begins to break down and turn into smoke. If you use an oil with too low of a smoke point on high heat, it will not only taste bad but also be unhealthy due to the oxidation process that takes place when exposed to extreme temperatures.

Knowing the smoke points for each type of oil helps ensure that you are using the right oil for your specific needs.

Finally, there are many health benefits associated with cooking with different types of oils depending on what they are made from and how they are processed.

Salt is one of the most used ingredients in cooking and it enhances flavors by bringing out more of their natural sweetness or bitterness. The right amount of salt can bring balance and depth to dishes. When using salt, it is important to start small and gradually add more until you reach your desired level of flavor.

> **Gamechanger:**
> Sautéing vegetables would require an oil with a higher smoke point like avocado or peanut oil, while shallow frying something like fish may call for vegetable or sunflower oil.

AVOCADO OIL

Avocado oil is great for high-heat cooking thanks to its high smoke point (520°F). It also has a mild flavor and a light texture that makes it ideal for marinades and salad dressings.

OLIVE OIL

Olive oil is one of the most popular types of cooking oils out there. It has a strong flavor and can be used in both high-heat and low heat applications (depending on how you want the dish to taste). It also has a moderate smoke point (375°F).

SESAME OIL

Sesame oil has a nutty, aromatic flavor that goes well with Asian dishes like stir fries and noodle bowls. This oil should always be used towards the end of the cooking process because its low smoke point (350°F) means it can burn easily when exposed to high temperatures.

CANOLA AND VEGETABLE OIL

These two types of oil are very similar and are often used interchangeably in recipes. They both have neutral flavors and high smoke points (400°F), making them ideal for deep frying and sautéing.

COCONUT OIL

Coconut oil is a great choice if you're looking for an alternative to traditional cooking oils. Its unique flavor adds an extra layer of complexity to dishes, but keep in mind that coconut oil has a relatively low smoke point (350°F) so it's best used at lower temperatures or towards the end of the cooking process.

PEANUT OIL

Peanut oil has an intense flavor that makes it perfect for Asian dishes like stir fries or noodle bowls. Its high smoke point (450°F) makes it suitable for deep frying as well as sautéing.

BUTTER AND LARD

Butter and lard both have their uses in cooking, but they should be used sparingly due to their relatively low smoke points (250°F - 375°F). They both add rich flavors but should only be used in dishes where they won't be exposed to high temperatures for too long.

HOW TO UNDERSTAND & FOLLOW A RECIPE

Following recipes can be intimidating, especially if you're new to cooking. However, following a recipe doesn't have to be scary or difficult! With the right approach, you can learn how to follow a recipe in no time.

READ THE RECIPE CLOSELY - DON'T JUST SKIM

It's important that you read the entire recipe before attempting it—don't just skim it! Make sure you understand all the instructions before beginning. Check out any unfamiliar cooking terms (use the glossary above!) so that you know what they mean before starting. This will save time and prevent confusion later in the process.

FIGURE OUT YOUR TIMING AND INGREDIENTS

Before getting started, take some time to make sure that you have all your ingredients and tools ready. This is also a good time to think through the timeline of when each step needs to be done. Will something need to chill overnight? Should something simmer for an hour? Take note of these details so that you can plan ahead properly.

PLAN AHEAD

Even if everything looks like it should be ready within an hour or two, plan ahead for potential challenges or delays—these things happen when cooking! If something needs to chill overnight (or even for several hours), take that into account as you plan your timeline.

Also, don't forget about clean-up. Allow enough time for washing dishes or wiping down countertops once everything is finished cooking.

MAKE NOTES

As you cook, keep notes about anything interesting or unique about how the dish tasted or looked. These notes will help inform future recipes. Did something need more salt? Was there too much liquid? All these details are useful as reference points for future meals.

LAY OUT YOUR TOOLS

Gather all your necessary tools before beginning so that they're close at hand when needed. This way, nothing gets missed in the shuffle! Have measuring spoons and cups easily accessible while mixing ingredients together. Likewise, have utensils nearby while stirring sauces on the stovetop.

10 Basic Recipes You Can Try

Here are a few basic recipes to whip up!

SPAGHETTI AND MEATBALLS

Spaghetti and meatballs is an Italian classic that's sure to be a hit with the family.

INGREDIENTS:

For the spaghetti: 1 lb spaghetti, Salt, 1 tbsp olive oil, 4 cups water.

For the meatballs: 1 lb ground beef, 1/2 cup breadcrumbs, 1/4 cup milk,
1/4 cup grated Parmesan cheese, 1/4 cup chopped fresh parsley, 1 egg
1 tsp salt, 1/2 tsp black pepper, 1/4 tsp garlic powder.

+ 1 bottle of tomato sauce.

DIRECTIONS:

Start by preheating your oven to 375 degrees Fahrenheit and then combining the ground beef, breadcrumbs, Parmesan cheese, garlic salt and eggs in a medium bowl.

Mix well and form into 1-inch balls; place them on a greased baking sheet. Bake in the oven for 15 minutes or until golden brown.

In the meantime, bring a large pot of salted water to boil over high heat; add spaghetti noodles and cook until they are al dente (about 10 minutes). Drain noodles in a colander; return them to the same pot used for boiling and stir in tomato sauce and red pepper flakes.

Heat through over low heat for about 5 minutes before serving with meatballs on top. Drizzle olive oil over each plate before serving if desired.

PASTA PRIMAVERA

This one-pot pasta dish is perfect for busy weeknights when you don't have much time to cook but still want something tasty.

INGREDIENTS:

olive oil, garlic cloves, onions, any type of pasta of your choice (penne or fettuccine work great), frozen vegetables like peas or corn, canned tomatoes, parmesan cheese (optional), and basil leaves (also optional).

DIRECTIONS:

Get out your biggest pot and heat some olive oil over medium heat before adding the chopped garlic cloves and diced onions for about 5 minutes until they soften up. Then add in the frozen vegetables of your choice along with canned tomatoes (juices included!), plus some salt and pepper if desired.

Let this simmer uncovered for 10 minutes before stirring in uncooked pasta noodles—you should also fill the pot up with water so that there's enough liquid to cook the noodles all the way through without drying out your sauce—then bring to a boil before reducing heat to low-medium while continuing to stir occasionally until everything is cooked through nicely (about 8 minutes).

When finished cooking, sprinkle on top freshly grated parmesan cheese or sliced basil leaves for added flavor! Enjoy!

GRILLED CHEESE SANDWICH

This classic sandwich couldn't be easier

INGREDIENTS:

two slices of bread (white or wheat), butter or margarine (for spreading), cheese slices (cheddar or American) and a non-stock skillet set over medium heat.

DIRECTIONS:

Start by spreading one side of each slice of bread with butter or margarine; place one slice of bread in the pan butter side down and lay one slice of cheese on top; cover with the remaining slice of bread butter side up. Let cook until bread is golden brown on both sides (about 2-3 minutes per side).

Flip the sandwich carefully so that the cheese melts evenly throughout the sandwich (you may need to reduce heat slightly). Serve the sandwich hot out of the pan with ketchup if desired!

CHEESY CHICKEN QUESADILLAS

Who doesn't love a good quesadilla?

INGREDIENTS:

4 flour tortillas, 2 cups shredded chicken breast (cooked), 1 cup mozzarella cheese (shredded) , ¼ cup chopped cilantro leaves (optional).

DIRECTIONS:

Heat up a skillet over medium heat then place one tortilla onto the pan followed by ¼ cup shredded chicken breast scattered evenly across the surface followed by ¼ cup mozzarella cheese topped with cilantro leaves if desired. Then top with another tortilla, pressing lightly so it sticks together. Allow the quesadilla to cook on each side for 3 minutes or until golden brown.

Remove from the pan then repeat the process until all four quesadillas have been made then cut each one into quarters using a knife or pizza cutter before serving! Enjoy!

PANCAKES

Everyone loves pancakes! And it is ok to make yourself pancakes for supper. Don't let anyone tell you differently!

INGREDIENTS:

1 cup all-purpose flour, 2 tbsp granulated sugar,
2 tsp baking powder, 1/2 tsp salt, 1 cup milk,
1 large egg, 2 tbsp unsalted butter,
melted 1 tsp vanilla extract, Butter or oil for cooking

DIRECTIONS:

In a large bowl mix together flour, baking powder and salt then whisk in the sugar followed by milk/almond milk until the batter is smooth; fold in any extra ingredients you desire at this point like blueberries or banana slices if using them!

Heat the griddle/pan over medium-high heat until hot enough that drops of water sizzle when sprinkled onto it; lightly grease the griddle/pan with melted butter/vegetable oil then spoon the pancake batter onto the griddle/pan into desired size pancakes.

Cook pancakes on each side until golden brown then serve immediately while still warm topped with syrup or honey if desired!

SCRAMBLED EGGS

Scrambled eggs are simple and delicious.

INGREDIENTS:

butter, eggs, milk (optional), salt, and pepper for seasoning.

DIRECTIONS:

Start by cracking two eggs into a bowl and whisking them until the yolks and whites are combined. Then add in some milk (if desired) for extra fluffiness—plus a pinch of salt and pepper for flavor.

Heat a pan over medium heat with butter or oil and pour the egg mixture in. Stir occasionally with a spatula until the eggs are cooked through—usually about

3 minutes or so—and voila! Serve with toast for a hearty breakfast that will keep you full until lunch time.

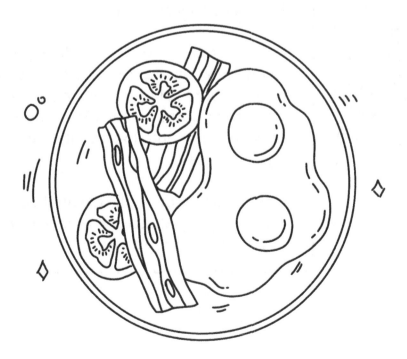

Chapter 10:
Get Er' Done!
Cleaning and Sorting

It can be hard to stay organized and keep your space clean.
I know this firsthand because I was guilty of not doing either until recently.

I was always overwhelmed by the idea of tackling such a daunting task, so instead, I put it off for as long as possible. However, it wasn't until I got serious about my organization that I realized how much difference it made in my day-to-day life. And believe it or not, by spending just a few minutes each day cleaning and organizing your space, you can avoid that overwhelm and get way more done.

First off, let's simplify what needs to be done to take care of your space or home.

Cleaning or Chores: When we clean, the point is to take away dirt, dust, grim and bacteria [among other nasty things] that may have been building up in a particular place in the house. By cleaning, we are ensuring that the space that we live in is safe and healthy for all the people who live there. In most households, each person living in the home has a responsibility to help with cleaning the home.

Organization: When we organize, we assign a particular 'home or space' for each object in our home so that it is easy for everyone to find it when they need it. If you know where your things are you'll be able to spend time doing things you want to do instead of wasting time trying to find them. In most households, the mother or father has the primary responsibility for organizing the home and determining where items go. Still, it is the responsibility of everyone living there to return items to their proper place out of respect for the other people living there.

Fixing Stuff: Most households have at least one person who has been assigned the 'role of keeping parts of the house in working order. For example, if the toilet is clogged, usually there is a person who is routinely called upon to fix it. If you know that you are good at fixing things, think about offering up your services if you haven't already done so.

WHAT TYPE OF CLEANER ARE YOU?

Procrastinator: I put it off until my room stinks.

Never-Get-to-it At all: Not only do I procrastinate, but I also just don't ever do it at all. This usually annoys my parents.

I'm OCD: I get to cleaning right away and am stressed out when I leave a space dirty.

Moody: If I'm in the mood to look after my space, I will.

Don't fit in any of these categories? Get Specific here:

_____

_____

| Procastinator | Never-get-to it-at all | I'm OCD | Moody |

A BRIEF GUIDE TO CLEANERS:

Having a clean home is essential for maintaining a healthy and comfortable living space. However, with so many different types of household cleaners available, it can be overwhelming to decide which ones to use for specific areas of your home.

Here's a breakdown:

Window Cleaners:

Window cleaners are specifically designed to remove dirt, dust, and grime from glass surfaces. They are available in both spray and wipe formats. Most window cleaners are made with a formula that does not leave streaks or residues on surfaces. Window cleaners are safe to use on all types of glass, including mirrors and shower doors.

Tile Cleaners:

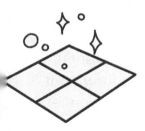

Tile cleaners are perfect for cleaning any type of tile surfaces in your home. They work by breaking down dirt and grease that accumulate in tiles, which are difficult to remove with regular cleaning solutions. Tile cleaners are formulated to clean grout lines and remove any stains from tile surfaces. Some tile cleaners are available in both spray and wipe format, while some come in easy to apply scrubbing solutions.

Wood Cleaners:

Wood cleaners are specifically formulated to clean and protect wooden surfaces. These cleaners replenish the natural oils in wooden surfaces and provide protection from dirt, stains, and water. Wood cleaners are made to maintain the beauty and natural look of wood by removing dirt and grime without damaging the surface. They are perfect for cleaning wooden floors, furniture, and countertops.

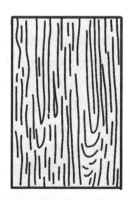

Floor Cleaners:

Floor cleaners are designed to clean different types of flooring surfaces, such as hardwood, laminate, and tile. They work by dissolving dirt and grime that accumulate on floors, leaving the surface clean and shiny. Most floor cleaners are formulated to be safe for use in homes with children and pets. They are available in both mop and bucket formulas or spray and wipe formats.

Bathroom Cleaners:

Bathroom cleaners are designed to clean and sanitize bathroom surfaces such as sinks, toilets, and showers. They work by dissolving soap scum, grime, and mineral deposits. Most bathroom cleaners are formulated to kill germs and bacteria that accumulate in most bathroom surfaces. They come in different formulas such as foam, gel, and spray format to suit different cleaning needs.

Mold/ Mildew Cleaners:

Mold or mildew are fungal growths that form on damp surfaces in your home. They can cause respiratory problems and allergies if left untreated. Mold and mildew cleaners are designed to remove mold and prevent it from forming again. They work by killing the fungi that form mold and mildew. Most mold and mildew cleaners are available in spray and wipe format.

All-Purpose Cleaners:

All-purpose cleaners are designed to be used on multiple surfaces and for different cleaning purposes. They work by dissolving dirt, grime, and stains from various surfaces, such as countertops, floors, walls, and appliances. All-purpose cleaners are formulated to be safe for use in homes with children and pets. They come in different formulas such as aerosol, spray, and wipes to suit different cleaning needs.

SAFETY WHEN USING CLEANERS

Cleaning is an essential part of our daily lives, but we often forget about the risks involved with handling cleaning products. Common household cleaners contain harmful chemicals that, when improperly handled, can cause health problems. That's why it's important to take the necessary precautions to keep yourself safe.

Here are five tips:

Always wear protective gear before handling any cleaning product. Be sure to wear proper protective equipment. This includes gloves, eye protection, and a face mask if necessary. These items will protect your skin, eyes, and respiratory system from harmful chemicals.

Read the label. It's essential to read the label of the cleaner you're using to understand the potential hazards and how to properly use it. This includes reading the instructions on how to use the product, the warning labels, and symbols: and any first aid information if the cleaner is accidentally ingested or comes into contact with skin.

Keep cleaners out of reach of children and pets. Many cleaning products contain chemicals that can be harmful if swallowed, inhaled, or even touched. Young children and pets are prone to accidents, so be sure to store cleaners in a locked cabinet or at a height that is not accessible to them.

Do not mix cleaners. It can be tempting to mix cleaners to create a stronger cleaning solution, but it is a dangerous practice that can lead to chemical reactions that cause harm to you, others, and the environment. Each cleaner is designed to work alone, so never mix two cleaners together.

Once you've finished cleaning, it's important to dispose of the cleaning product properly. Follow the instructions on the label or research the proper way to dispose of it in your community. It may not be safe or legal to pour cleaning chemicals down the drain, so it's important to take the time to properly dispose of them.

DEFINE WHAT "CLEAN" MEANS TO YOU

Everyone has different standards of what "clean" looks like, so start by defining this for yourself. When deciding how often you should clean certain areas of your home or what kind of products you want to use, think about what matters to you.

Do you prefer natural cleaning solutions? Is dusting every week too often? Are there certain areas that are of higher priority than others? Defining your own cleaning standards will help make your routines faster and more effective.

ON A SCALE FROM 1-10, HOW CLEAN AND TIDY DO YOU THINK YOU ARE?

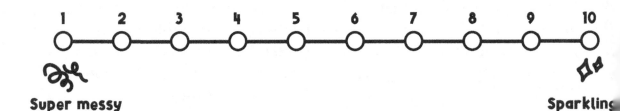

| 1 | 2 | 3 | 4 | 5 | 6 | 7 | 8 | 9 | 10 |

Super messy   Sparkling

DO YOUR PARENTS ENCOURAGE YOU TO BE CLEAN, OR DO THEY SEEM NOT TO CARE?

IF YOU ANSWERED YES, WHAT DO THEY OFTEN ASK YOU TO DO?

Now, take a second to think about your personal cleanliness standards. Describe the level of clean that makes you comfortable and happy.

WHAT DOES CLEAN MEAN TO YOU? WRITE IT DOWN BELOW:

_____
_____
_____
_____
_____

WHICH OF THE FOLLOWING 'ROOMS HAS BEEN CLEANED UP?
[CIRCLE ONE]

COMMON CLEANING TERMS YOU MIGHT ENCOUNTER

HERE ARE SOME COMMON CLEANING TERMS YOU MIGHT ENCOUNTER:

▷ **Antibacterial** - This term refers to any product or technique that kills bacteria on surfaces. It's important to use antibacterial products when cleaning to keep germs away from your family and pets.

▷ **Cleaning** - This is the act of removing dirt, germs, and other impurities from surfaces to make them safe and hygienic. Many people use a variety of different cleaning products and techniques for this purpose.

▷ **Decluttering** - Decluttering means getting rid of items that are no longer needed or wanted to create more space in your home. Decluttering can help make it easier to find things when you need them, as well as improve the overall aesthetic of your home.

▷ **Decontamination** - Decontamination is the process of removing any hazardous materials from a surface or area before cleaning it. This may involve using special equipment such as masks and gloves to protect yourself from any potential harm.

▷ **Deep cleaning** - Deep cleaning is a comprehensive form of cleaning that involves scrubbing all surfaces and vacuuming carpets to get rid of dirt, dust, allergens, and other particles that have accumulated over time. Deep cleaning is typically done once every few months or so but may be done more often depending on lifestyle factors like pet ownership or allergies.

▷ **Disinfect** - Disinfecting is an antibacterial method used for killing harmful bacteria on surfaces with chemicals or heat treatment (such as boiling water). It's important to disinfect areas regularly to maintain a safe and healthy environment inside your home.

- **Dwell Time** - Dwell time refers to the amount of time that a particular disinfectant needs to be left on a surface for it to kill off all germs present on the surface effectively. Different products have different dwell times, so it's important to check the label before using any product for maximum effectiveness!

- **Sanitize** - Sanitizing is like disinfecting but uses fewer chemicals than disinfectants do. This makes sanitizing safer for both humans and pets alike since there are fewer harsh chemicals involved in the process. Sanitizing is typically used on food-contact surfaces such as kitchen countertops or dishware after they have already been cleaned with soap and water.

- **HEPA** - HEPA stands for High-Efficiency Particulate Air filters; these filters are designed specifically for catching small particles such as dust mites, pollen grains, mold spores, etc., which helps reduce allergic reactions by reducing airborne irritants inside homes with poor ventilation systems. HEPA filters should be changed regularly according to manufacturer recommendations to maintain their effectiveness at trapping small particles out of air circulation inside homes.

- **Microfiber** - Microfiber cloths are made up of tiny fibers which trap dirt particles better than regular cloths do; they also require less water since they absorb liquid quickly instead of leaving streaks behind like regular clothes might do when wetted down with water/cleaning solutions wiping activities (e.g., dusting counters/tabletops).

- **Green cleaning** - Green cleaning refers specifically to using natural ingredients such as vinegar or baking soda instead of chemical-based products when dealing with everyday household chores. Green cleaners are eco-friendly because they don't contain any harsh toxins which could pollute our environment if disposed of improperly into oceans and groundwater.

SO, WHAT EXACTLY NEEDS TO BE DONE?

Let me set the scene:

it's a beautiful Saturday morning, the sun is shining, and the birds are chirping. But instead of enjoying the day, I was stuck inside doing chores with my mom. We had a long list of tasks to accomplish, including dusting, vacuuming, washing the windows, and scrubbing the bathrooms. I was not motivated to help, but my mom insisted that it was important for me to learn how to clean and take care of a home.

And boy, was she right.

We started in the living room, and I quickly realized that there was dust everywhere. Like, seriously, everywhere. We had to move all the furniture and vacuum under it, then dust all the surfaces.

My mom showed me how to use different cleaning products and tools to get everything sparkling clean. But even after all that work, I couldn't help but notice that there were still spots that we missed. Cleaning is a never-ending task.

Next up was the kitchen. Now, I'm no stranger to washing dishes, but I didn't realize how many different surfaces needed to be cleaned. We wiped down the counters, cabinets, and fridge, scrubbed the oven and stove, and even mopped the floor. And that was just the kitchen!

We still had two bathrooms and three bedrooms to tackle.

By the time we finished cleaning the last room, I was exhausted. But as I looked around and saw how clean everything was, I felt a sense of pride in what we had accomplished. And I also felt a newfound appreciation for all the hard work that my parents do on a daily basis to keep our home clean and comfortable.

DAILY TASKS:

VACUUM RUGS & CARPETS

Vacuuming daily helps keep dirt and dust from accumulating around your house. This makes it easier for bigger messes to clean up quickly since there won't be a layer of dirt beneath them. Vacuuming also helps reduce allergens in your home which is great for anyone who has allergies or asthma. Plus, it's much faster than sweeping!

CLEAN THE TOILET

It might seem like you're overdoing it if you're cleaning your toilet every day, but think of it this way: you don't want your friend to come over and be witness to your not so pleasant toilet, do you? Just take a few minutes each day to spray down your toilet with some cleaner; scrub it with a brush if necessary, and wipe it down with some paper towels or a rag.

Doing this daily prevents dirt and grime from building up over time which makes deep cleaning much less of a hassle later.

DON'T FORGET TO DUST

Dust can accumulate quickly in any home, so it's important not to forget about it when cleaning! Dusting regularly can help reduce allergens in the air while keeping surfaces looking fresh and new. A microfiber cloth is perfect for grabbing dust without using harsh chemicals, plus they come in lots of fun colors!

DECLUTTER EVERY DAY

Clutter can pile up pretty quickly if you don't take care of it right away. Get into the habit of decluttering daily rather than waiting until everything has built up—this will prevent messes from getting out of hand later. Throwing things away or donating them when they're no longer needed is also great for reducing stress levels since clutter can be overwhelming when left unchecked!

LAUNDRY

The moment your laundry basket starts overflowing with clothes, you know it's time to do your laundry. Instead of waiting for your clothes to get moldy or smell funky, make it a daily routine to sort your clothes and follow up with their washing.

Every day, take a few minutes to sort through your clothes, set aside the dirty ones, and toss the rest in their respective drawers. Setting aside five to ten minutes each day can make the task less daunting and less time-consuming.

DISHES & TIDYING THE KITCHEN

The kitchen is one of the busiest and messiest areas in your home. Dirty dishes, cluttered countertops, and scattered cooking utensils can make your kitchen look like a complete disaster.

To avoid this, take a few minutes out of your day to tidy up your kitchen after each meal you have. Start by putting any leftovers away and then wash or rinse any items you used while cooking. You can use the sponge in your sink to clean up any spills, crumbs, or greases on the countertops or stove. This will help maintain a clean and organized kitchen.

WEEKLY CLEANING

CLEAN THE WINDOWS AND MIRRORS

Windows and mirrors should be cleaned regularly to remove dirt, fingerprints, and smudges. Make sure to use lint-free cloths for cleaning glass surfaces so that there won't be any streaks left behind after you wipe them down! And if you want extra shine on those windows or mirrors, try using a bit of vinegar in warm water for an added sparkle.

MOP THE FLOORS

Floors can quickly accumulate dirt, dust, and grime from your shoes, pets, and food spills. It's not pleasant to walk on dirty floors, so it's important to mop them regularly. Sweeping or vacuuming your floors a few times a week is good practice.

Still, mopping at least once a week will make sure you're getting rid of all the dirt and dust that has accumulated. If you have pets, mop twice a week to get rid of any hair or pet particles that might irritate your allergies. Mopping is an important part of keeping your living space clean and avoiding allergies or illnesses.

CLEAN THE BATHROOMS

Bathrooms are some of the dirtiest places in the house. All the moisture and steam from the showers and baths create environments for germs and mildew to thrive. That's why it's essential to clean your bathrooms regularly.

Clean and sanitize your toilet, sink, and shower every week. Pay attention to any mold or mildew that might be growing in the tub or shower corners. Get rid of it with a bathroom cleaner using a scrub brush. Don't forget to wash your bathroom rugs and towels weekly too.

DON'T FORGET TO WASH THE LINENS

One of the most important things to remember when it comes to cleaning is to wash your linens regularly. This includes sheets, pillowcases, towels, and any other fabric items that come into contact with your body or surfaces in your house.

Regularly washing linens ensure that germs don't build up and spread throughout your home. Aim to wash these items every two weeks or so for best results.

EVERYTHING YOU NEED TO KNOW TO KEEP YOUR ROOM CLEAN

Your room is your domain. That means you should consider yourself primarily responsible for keeping it clean, and tidy and ensuring it is a healthy space for you to live in.

WHEN YOU ARE CLEANING YOUR ROOM, WHAT DO YOU USUALLY CLEAN?

_____

_____

_____

_____

_____

_____

TAKE A LOOK AT YOUR LIST ABOVE, AND SEE IF THESE WERE MENTIONED:

- Wipe your mirror.

- Dust off your dresser.

- Declutter any surfaces, floors, and closets. One easy way to organize your cluttered mess is to make three piles: a) trash, b) donate, and c) put away.

- Make your bed. Ensure that your pillowcase and sheets are clean and that they don't smell.

- Take all of your dirty laundry to the laundry room, and if you're feeling extra motivated [and if there is enough dirty clothes] start a load.

- Take your trash out.

- Wash your dirty dishes.

HERE ARE SOME TIPS THAT WILL MAKE CLEANING YOUR ROOM A LOT EASIER:

KEEP A GARBAGE CAN IN YOUR ROOM

Having a garbage can in your room makes it easy for you to throw away rubbish without having to leave the room or take out the trash every day. Make sure to empty it regularly, though, so it doesn't become too full! This hack will help keep your room clean and free from clutter too!

DON'T EAT IN YOUR BEDROOM

Eating in your bedroom can quickly create a cluttered mess. Not only are there crumbs everywhere, but also wrappers and containers. Eating outside of the bedroom makes it much easier to keep your bedroom clean and tidy! So, remember: no eating in bed!

TAKE CARE OF YOUR CLOTHES IMMEDIATELY

As soon as you remove an article of clothing, put it away in its designated place. If there is a stain on the item or if it needs to be washed, attend to those tasks right away instead of waiting until later. This way you won't have piles of dirty clothes lying around, and you won't forget about them either!

LOOK UNDER YOUR BED

If after you've cleaned your room, you still notice a stink in your room, make sure that you've looked under your bed for any dirty laundry, dishes, or trash that may have found its way under there.

AIR IT OUT

If it still stinks in your room, open a window.

YOUR CLEANING PLAN

The best way to stay on top of your cleaning is by creating a plan or schedule that works for you. Set aside certain days of the week or certain times of the day when you will do specific tasks, such as laundry, vacuuming, dusting, etc., so that everything gets done in an orderly manner.

This way, it won't feel like such an overwhelming task because it is spread out over time. It also ensures that nothing gets missed or forgotten about.

WRITE DOWN YOUR CLEANING PLAN BELOW:

Monday:

Tuesday:

Wednesday:

Thursday:

Friday:

Saturday:

Sunday:

ORGANIZING YOUR SPACE

Organizing your space has more benefits than just being aesthetically pleasing. It can also help reduce stress, boost productivity, promote mental clarity, and improve overall well-being. When you are surrounded by clutter or chaos, it can be difficult to focus on the task at hand or even think clearly.

Having an organized space allows you to quickly locate what you need without searching through piles of stuff. It can also be therapeutic: the physical act of decluttering and sorting is almost like meditation—it helps clear your mind and gives you a sense of accomplishment when you're done.

Organizing your space isn't just about tidying up occasionally. It's also about developing good habits that will help you to stay organized in the long run. This means taking the time each day to put things back where they belong after using them and setting aside time each week for cleaning tasks like dusting, vacuuming, etc.

It might seem like an extra chore in the beginning, but once you get into the habit of taking care of your environment, these tasks will become second nature and won't feel tedious anymore.

When it comes to staying organized long-term, creating systems is key. Invest in storage solutions that fit with your lifestyle—whether that means colorful baskets for toys or filing cabinets for paperwork. And label everything clearly so that everyone knows where things belong when not in use.

Set aside 10-15 minutes every week just for decluttering — this could mean donating old clothes or textbooks, throwing away broken items, or getting rid of anything else that has accumulated over time. This is also a great opportunity for a deep clean if necessary!

DON'T FORGET ABOUT HOME MAINTENANCE

Home maintenance should also be part of your regular cleaning routine! Take some time each month to do basic household maintenance tasks like changing air filters, checking smoke detectors, vacuuming furniture and carpets, etc. Having a checklist handy will help you keep track of what needs to be done each month, so nothing falls through the cracks!

Many of these tasks are not those you'll want to tackle unless you are a homeowner. If you're still living with your parents, in an apartment, or aren't comfortable with certain maintenance tasks, you'll want to outsource them (for example, hire an HVAC technician to clean your furnace filter).

Nevertheless, the checklist below has some tasks you'll want to keep in mind, particularly as you grow up and move out of your parent's house.

HOME MAINTENANCE CHECKLIST

- Not Clean furnace filters
- Check water softener
- Inspect tub and sink drains; unclog if necessary
- Test smoke alarms and carbon monoxide detectors
- Inspect electrical cords for wear and tear. Replace
- Vacuum heat vents and registers
- Flush hot water from the water heater to remove sediment
- Clean the garbage disposal
- Seal cracks and gaps in windows and doors
- Touch up paint

- Rake leaves and aerate lawn
- Inspect roofing for missing or damaged singles
- Drain and winterize exterior plumbing
- Clean the carpets
- Clean door and window screens
- Power wash windows and siding
- Vacuum exhaust fan grills
- Vacuum refrigerator and freezer coils
- Defrost freezer
- Chance air conditioner filter
- Polish wood furniture
- Inspect and pump septic tank (hire a professional for this)
- Remove lint from dryer vent
- Inspect caulking
- Clean kitchen exhaust fan filter
- Check dishwasher for leaks
- Seal tile grout
- Prune trees and shrubs

RECYCLING

Recycling is a process of taking materials or products that are no longer in use and breaking them down into something new. This helps keep waste out of landfills and reduces the need for more natural resources, which can help protect the environment.

Plus, the items you recycle can be used to make other things like furniture, clothing, bags, and even art! So, when you recycle something, you're not just throwing it away—you're giving it a second life in another form.

Recycling has lots of benefits for our planet. By reducing the amount of waste going into landfills (where garbage sits for years), we can reduce air pollution and conserve energy. And by breaking down materials like plastic or paper into something new, we conserve natural resources like oil that would otherwise be needed to make those same items from scratch.

Personally, I started recycling to do my part in protecting the environment and teaching my kids about sustainability. Every week, my family goes through our trash to separate recyclables from non-recyclables before heading out on our weekly curbside pickup day. It doesn't take long but is an important reminder that every little bit helps!

WHAT CAN BE RECYCLED?

Recycling is a great way to reduce your environmental impact. It's also an easy way to help create positive change in the world. But what can be recycled? There are a lot of misconceptions out there, so let's look at what you can and can't recycle.

E-WASTE

E-waste or electronic waste includes items like computers, cell phones, printers, and other electronics that contain hazardous materials such as lead, mercury, and cadmium.

These materials should never be thrown away in the garbage: instead, they should be taken to e-waste facilities where they will be recycled properly and safely.

PAPER

Paper products like magazines, newspapers, paper bags, cardboard boxes and even pizza boxes can all be recycled. In fact, paper products make up about 40 percent of the total waste stream in the United States!

Gamechanger:
When it comes to recycling paper products, make sure that it is not contaminated with food or liquids as these can contaminate other recyclable materials when processed.

PLASTIC

Most plastic packaging, such as bottles, containers, and lids, can all be recycled. However, some plastic items like laminates (e.g., coatings on beverage cartons) cannot be recycled because they are too difficult for recycling plants to process efficiently.

GLASS

Glass is one of the most widely recycled materials around the world due to its ability to be melted down repeatedly without losing its structural integrity or purity.

ALUMINUM CANS

Aluminum cans are one of the most widely recycled items around the world thanks to their lightweight properties which makes them much cheaper to transport than other metals such as steel or copper.

If they aren't contaminated with food or liquid, they can easily be recycled over and over again with minimal energy expenditure needed by recycling plants during processing.

CARDBOARD

Cardboard boxes are one of the most common items found in curbside bins around the world due to their ability to be broken down into small pieces which helps reduce their overall volume when transported for recycling purposes.

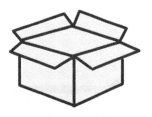

TIPS FOR RECYCLING

The first rule of the recycling club – reduce the number of products you buy, use, and throw away. One of the simplest ways to make a dent in the amount of waste you create is to buy and use fewer items.

Make it as easy as possible to separate recyclables from other trash by having dedicated bins throughout the house. Place recycling bins in convenient and accessible areas, like near your trash can, in your room, and in your bathroom. Clear, easy-to-read labels can help remind everyone what goes where.

Not all recycling programs are created equal, so it's essential to know what materials can be recycled in your area. Common recyclable items include cans, bottles, books, metal, aluminum, glass, newspapers, and electronics.

Find creative ways to reuse things around your home. Get inspired and transform old clothes into shopping bags, rags, or even funky new clothing pieces. Repurpose used containers for crafts, storage, or planters. The possibilities are endless, and you'll be diverting waste from landfills while giving new life to old items.

Make simple, eco-friendly swaps in your daily routine. Turn off the water when brushing your teeth or use a washcloth instead of disposable paper napkins. Unplug chargers when not in use and switch to energy-efficient light bulbs. Small changes in your everyday habits can lead to big differences in your overall environmental impact.

There are a lot of rules and regulations that come along with it, so it's easy to make mistakes if you don't know what you're doing. Here's a list of what not to do when it comes to recycling:

- **Try to recycle broken glasses and bottles**. These should be thrown away because they could potentially injure workers at the recycling center or contaminate other materials.

- **Throw yard waste into recycling bins**. Grass clippings and leaves should be hauled away at the next brush pick up date or placed in a green yard waste container that some cities have.

- **Try to recycle waxed cardboard or Styrofoam**. These items cannot be recycled due to the coating they have on them which prevents them from being broken down properly.

- **Recycle pizza boxes**. Even though they are made from cardboard, they usually contain grease and food particles which makes them non-recyclable.

- **Recycle auto parts, plumbing parts or any combination of metal and paper**. These can't be recycled because they contain hazardous materials like lead, oil, etc.

- **Put trash in the recycling bin**. This can make the entire load into the trash, which defeats the purpose of recycling altogether! Some cities will even charge you an extra fee if they catch you doing this.

- **Recycle mirrors, fluorescent tubes, light bulbs, or safety glass.** These items contain hazardous materials like mercury and must be disposed of properly by taking them to a local hazardous waste facility for proper disposal.

- **Recycle food.** Food can be composted but it cannot be recycled since it contains organic matter that needs to break down before it can be reused in any way shape or form.

LAUNDRY TIPS

Doing laundry is one of those adulting chores that can seem daunting. When I was in high school, I remember being overwhelmed by the thought of doing my own laundry. And yet, with just a few tips and tricks, I quickly learned how to take control of this task.

SORT

The first step to laundry success is understanding the basics of sorting your clothes. Start by separating your items into three piles: whites, colors, and delicates. This helps ensure that any colors don't bleed onto your whites and cause staining.

Be sure to sort these piles into two fabric types: cotton (like t-shirts) and synthetics (like polyester). Washing synthetic fabrics together can cause them to pill—a common problem where small balls of fabric form on the surface due to friction between different materials.

DECODING LABELS

Pay attention to the tags on each piece of clothing as they provide valuable information about how to care for it properly. You might see a "W" or "X" on the tag which tells you whether it is safe to wash in the machine (the W) or dry clean only (the X).

Other symbols tell you how hot or cold the water should be used when washing or what kind of dryer cycle you should use when drying.

All of this information will help preserve your clothing longer and prevent damage from happening.

STAIN REMOVAL

It's inevitable that at some point while wearing one of your garments, it will become stained. But don't panic! There are several things you can do to remove stains without ruining the fabric.

For example, soak up excess liquids with a paper towel before applying soap directly onto the stain, then rinse with a damp cloth and allow it to air dry completely before throwing it in the wash.

Consider using vinegar or baking soda as natural alternatives to chemical-based cleaners; they work great!

WASHING

After sorting through all your items, carefully load them into the washer making sure not to overload it as this can cause uneven agitation during washing cycles which can damage fabrics negatively over time.

When adding detergent, use less than what is usually recommended since too much soap can leave residue behind after rinsing which may irritate sensitive skin types or cause an accumulation of dirt more quickly than normal on clothes over time.

Now it's time to pick which wash cycle is best for each pile of clothes. Generally speaking, you should use cold water for both delicates and colors: hot water can cause shrinking or fading in certain fabrics.

For cotton, like t-shirts, jeans, and towels, it's best practice to use warm water since it does a better job of removing dirt from these heavier fabrics than cold water does. Lastly, always pay attention to the instructions on your clothing labels so you know exactly how each garment should be washed!

DRYING

Once you've finished washing your clothes, it's important not to forget about drying them properly too! Again, make sure you read all care labels before putting anything in a dryer.

For example, some delicate fabrics should not go in the dryer at all—they are best air dried or line dried instead! If you're using a dryer for items like jeans or towels, remember that heat breaks down fibers faster so avoid over-drying these items if possible.

It also helps to separate heavy items from light ones while they're drying so they don't get tangled together during the cycle.

FOLDING

Once your clothes are done washing, it's time to tackle another dreaded task—folding! But don't worry: folding isn't as hard as it seems once you get the hang of it.

Start by laying out each garment flat on a surface so that all creases are smoothed out before folding them in half lengthwise twice, then folding each side inwards until all edges meet at the center of the garment—this will ensure that everything looks neat when hung up in your closet or drawer.

And don't forget to hang knits such as sweaters or delicate fabrics up instead of folding them so they maintain their shape over time!

USE THIS SPACE TO DRAW A PICTURE OF THE WASHING MACHINE THAT YOU USE AT HOME.
MAKE A NOTE OF THE DIALS AND SETTINGS THAT YOU USE.

QUICK GUIDE TO SEWING

For as long as I can remember, I've been fascinated by fabrics and fashion. When I finally decided to learn how to sew, it was a game-changer for me. Learning how to sew gave me the skills and confidence to create something of my very own. And now, I'm here to tell you why learning how to sew is a valuable life skill that everyone should have in their arsenal.

The first thing you need when learning how to sew is a sewing machine. If you don't want to invest in one right away, consider renting one or borrowing one from a family member or friend. Once you have your sewing machine, you'll need some basic supplies like thread, needles, fabric scissors, pins, fabric, and an iron. With these tools on hand, you're ready to get started!

Once you've gathered all the materials necessary for sewing projects, it's time to learn the basics of sewing. The first step is familiarizing yourself with your sewing machine and understanding its different functions and settings.

Once you understand the machine's capabilities, practice stitching lines on scrap fabric until you are comfortable with the machine's speed and motion. This will help prevent mistakes on your final project and make for an enjoyable experience overall. You'll also want to learn about different fabrics, such as cotton versus polyester versus satin, so that you can select the best fabric for each project.

Learning how to sew doesn't have to be intimidating or complicated; simple projects like mending clothes can easily be done with basic knowledge of sewing principles and techniques.

As your skills improve over time, try more complex projects like making clothing items such as skirts or shirts or even crafting accessories like bags or hats! Anything that requires stitching can be mastered over time—all it needs is practice!

WHY DO YOU WANT TO LEARN HOW TO SEW? WRITE DOWN A FEW OF YOUR GOALS AND "GOAL PROJECTS" BELOW:

_____
_____
_____
_____
_____
_____

LEARN TO STITCH BY HAND FIRST

Before you dive into learning how to use a sewing machine, take the time to learn basic hand stitching techniques such as running stitch, backstitch, and whip stitch. This will give you a better understanding of the basics of sewing before moving on to using a machine. Plus, if something goes wrong with your machine or if it breaks down, knowing how to hand sew will still allow you to complete whatever project you're working on.

START WITH A QUALITY MACHINE

It's important to invest in a quality machine so that your projects don't suffer from poor craftsmanship due to equipment malfunction. A quality machine also makes learning how to use it easier because they have more features and usually comes with tutorials and instructions that can help guide beginners through their first projects!

CREATE A COMFORTABLE WORKSPACE

Creating a comfortable workspace is essential for you to be successful when learning how to sew. Having all your supplies easily accessible will help prevent frustration while working on projects and allow for maximum focus during your creative process.

Make sure there's enough light so that you can clearly see what you're doing and be sure that your workspace is free of clutter so that nothing gets in the way while sewing!

DON'T BE AFRAID OF MISTAKES

No one starts off perfect at anything – including sewing! Don't be afraid of making mistakes. Instead, learn from them and move forward. It's totally normal for things not to go quite right when learning something new – this just means there's room for growth and improvement!

TRY NEW PROJECTS

The best way to gain experience is through practice – so don't be afraid to dive into different types of projects. Try out different techniques like appliquéd patches or quilting blocks. If it doesn't work out the first time around, just try again until it does! You never know what kind of amazing creations may come from stepping outside your comfort zone and trying something new every once in a while.

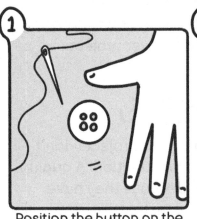

Position the button on the fabric.

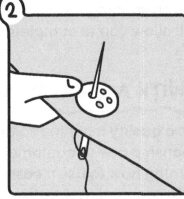

Push the threaded needle up through the fabric and through one hole in the button.

Push the needle down through the next hole and through the fabric.

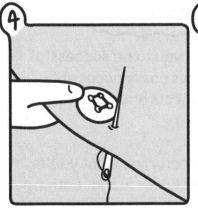

push the needle through the material, but not through a hole in the button.

Wrap the thread.

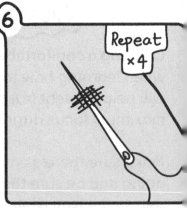

Make three or four stitches to secure the thread.

All in all, learning to properly clean for yourself and keep your home organized as a teen is no small feat. Having the ability to take responsibility for yourself and know how to use cleaning products effectively and efficiently can give you the confidence and skills to do other big things in life, like money management and home ownership.

We'll now move onto our next chapter - taking care of the business side of life. This will include exploring topics such as money management, employment opportunities, car ownership, housing options, and so much more! I'm excited about what we are about to learn and discover together.

So come along with me, and let's take the last leg of our journey together, one step at a time!

PART 3
Taking Care of Business

When I was a teenager, I remember how exciting it was to get my first job. I felt like an adult and couldn't wait to start earning money to pay for things and save up for the future. But what I didn't realize at the time was how important it would be to learn the basics of how to take care of business.

Just because you have the money, that doesn't mean you can spend it on whatever you want. It's important to understand where your money is going so you have enough to take care of the basics.

I remember when I got my first paycheck from my ice cream scooping job, I instantly ran to my favorite department store and bought three new pairs of jeans. That ate up not only the first paycheck but another $20 I had stashed in my wallet.

Before I knew it, a week's worth of hard work had disappeared down the drain.

Over time, I learned how to save my money - and make more of it - so that I didn't have to stress about unexpected expenses (like the time I had to pay for new brakes on my car).

Here are some tips to help you navigate everything from finding the perfect job to budgeting your money - and even paying your first bills as an adult.

Chapter 11:
The World of Work

I still remember the excitement and fear I felt when I applied for my first job. I was a teenager back then, trying to make a little extra pocket money. The idea of earning my own money, buying my own things, and being independent was very exciting but the thought of applying and standing out among a pile of other applicants was absolutely terrifying.

What if they don't like me? What if I look stupid? What if I don't get the job?

But, in the end, I gathered my courage and took a leap of faith. And guess what? I got the job!

I was successful in that first job interview, and while it built my confidence up immensely, it's important to note here that I've applied for many jobs since then and didn't always get the job.

You know what they say – if at first, you don't succeed, try, try again! Persistence is key when it comes to applying for a job.

In this chapter, we'll take a closer look at the different types of employment, as well as how to navigate the world of work.

TRADITIONAL EMPLOYMENT

As a teenager, you may already be feeling the pressure of trying to earn money for the things you want and need. Whether it's money for college, a new phone, or just a little extra spending cash, it's not always easy to find a job. I remember feeling frustrated when I was your age, spending hours filling out applications with no response.

Here are some tips.

BE STRATEGIC IN YOUR JOB SEARCH

It may seem like applying to every job opening you see is the best way to get hired, but it's not. Instead, focus on jobs that fit your skills and experience.

Before you start your job search, think about what type of work you would like to do. Consider your skills and interests and research jobs that align with them.

WRITE YOUR SKILLS AND INTERESTS BELOW, THEN MATCH THEM WITH JOBS THAT MIGHT FIT:

JOBS	SKILLS

For example, if you're good with kids, apply for babysitting or tutoring jobs. If you have an interest in fashion, look for retail jobs at clothing stores. By targeting your job search, you'll increase your chances of getting hired.

Before you apply for a job, it's important to know how many hours you can work. In most states, there are labor laws that limit the number of hours you can work and the times of day you can work.

Check with your state's labor department for more information. It's also important to consider your school schedule and extracurricular activities to ensure you can balance your work with your other commitments.

NETWORK WITH FRIENDS AND FAMILY

Word of mouth is a powerful tool, especially when it comes to finding a job. Let your friends and family know that you're looking for work and ask them to keep an ear out for job openings. You never know who might have a connection to a job that's a perfect fit.

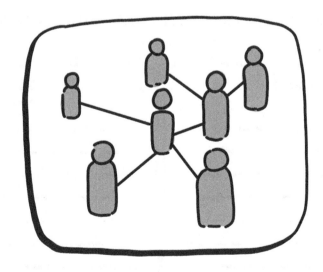

BUILD A STRONG RESUME

Even if you don't have much work experience, you can still create a strong resume. List any volunteer experience, school clubs, or hobbies that showcase your skills and interests. By highlighting these experiences, you'll show potential employers that you have a strong work ethic and are passionate about something.

Here are some resources you can use to help you craft the perfect resume:

Grammarly Resume Builder

Resume. Io

Zety

CRAFT THE PICTURE-PERFECT APPLICATION

When filling out applications, make sure to read the instructions carefully and provide accurate information. You may also want to create a resume that highlights your skills and experiences.
It's important to have a professional email address and voicemail greeting, as well as a wellwritten cover letter. Make sure to proofread everything several times before submitting.

Here's a checklist of what to include:

☐ **Personal Information:** Begin by providing your name, contact information, address, and email address. This information should be accurate, up-to-date, and professional. Make sure you have a professional email address such as john.doe@email.com instead of crazycatman@email.com. Keep in mind that this information is the first thing a hiring manager will see, so you want to make a good first impression.

☐ **Education:** Your education plays a crucial role in your job application process. Indicate your highest level of education in your resume, including the name of the institution, degree or diploma earned, and dates of attendance. Include any notable achievements or extracurricular activities that relate to your desired position. For example, if you're applying for a writing job, mention any writing competitions or journals you've been published in.

☐ **Experience:** Your work experience should highlight your skills and abilities that make you a fitting candidate for the position. You can list your previous employment history in reverse chronological order, starting with your most recent job. If you have little to no work experience, focus on your transferable skills and any relevant internships, volunteer work, or part-time jobs you've had.

☐ **Cover Letter:** A cover letter is an essential part of your job application. It's an opportunity to provide more details about your qualifications, work experience, and motivation behind applying for the job. In your cover letter, explain why you're the perfect candidate for the job and how you can add value to the company. Make sure you proofread your cover letter and customize it for each job you're applying for.

☐ **References:** Last but not least, provide a list of professional references. Your references should be people who know you well and can vouch for your character, work ethic, and other qualifications. They should include your former employers or colleagues, professors, or mentors who have worked closely with you.

Above all, be sure to customize.

Generic applications usually land in the reject pile. To capture an employer's attention, customize your application to suit the job description. Take time to read through the job requirements, tailor your resume and cover letter accordingly.

Show the employer that you understand the position and have relevant skills and qualities to offer. Highlight your most impressive accomplishments, such as academic or extra-curricular achievements.

PREPARE FOR JOB INTERVIEWS

Once you start getting job interviews, make sure you're prepared. Research the company you're interviewing with and practice answering common interview questions.

Dress appropriately for the job and arrive on time. Make sure to have a firm handshake and maintain eye contact.

By showing that you're serious about the job, you'll make a great impression on the hiring manager.

Here are some common interview questions you may be asked. Write out your answers to them below, then practice responding to them with a friend or family member.

1. "TELL US ABOUT YOURSELF."

This is a common icebreaker question that allows the interviewer to get to know you better. While it may seem easy, don't make the mistake of turning it into a life story. Keep your response to a minute, emphasizing your experience and skills that relate to the position.

For example, you can say something like, "I'm a recent graduate with a degree in marketing. My passion for social media marketing led me to intern at XYZ, where I learned how to create effective campaigns across multiple platforms."

WRITE YOUR SAMPLE RESPONSE HERE:

_____

_____

_____

_____

_____

_____

2. "WHY DO YOU WANT TO WORK FOR OUR COMPANY?"

This question is a way for the interviewer to see if you have done your homework and know about the company. Before the interview, research the company's mission, values, and competition. During the interview, be specific about how these align with your personal and professional goals.

For instance, "I've always been impressed by your company's commitment to innovation and sustainability. As someone who is passionate about making a positive impact in the world, I believe that working with a company that shares this value would be the best way to fulfill my personal and professional goals."

WRITE YOUR SAMPLE RESPONSE HERE:

_____
_____
_____
_____
_____
_____

3. "WHAT ARE YOUR STRENGTHS AND WEAKNESSES?"

This question aims to see if you know yourself and can reflect on your good and bad qualities honestly. While it may be tempting to pretend you don't have any weaknesses, that will not help you stand out.

Focus on one or two strengths that are relevant to the position and back them up with examples. As for weaknesses, identify those that are not essential to the job but show that you are working on improving them.

For instance, "I believe I have excellent communication skills. I have experience collaborating with different departments, and I can convey ideas and feedback clearly to everyone. As for weaknesses, sometimes, I tend to overthink, so I've been practicing mindfulness to be more present at the moment."

WRITE YOUR SAMPLE RESPONSE HERE:

_____
_____
_____
_____
_____

4. "CAN YOU TELL US ABOUT A TIME WHEN YOU HAD TO OVERCOME A CHALLENGE?"

This question focuses on your problem-solving and critical-thinking skills. The interviewer wants to see how you handle difficult situations and how you can learn from them. Prepare a story that demonstrates your ability to be resourceful, adaptable, and resilient.

For example, "When I worked as a volunteer at a summer camp, a severe thunderstorm caused a power outage. We had to think fast to evacuate the campers and relocate them to a safer place. We turned the situation into an opportunity to teach the campers how to adapt and take care of each other in a crisis."

WRITE YOUR SAMPLE RESPONSE HERE:

_____
_____
_____
_____

5. "DO YOU HAVE ANY QUESTIONS FOR US?"

This is your chance to show that you're interested in the company and the position.

Come prepared with a few questions about the company culture, work-life balance, or professional development opportunities. Avoid asking about salary or benefits in the first interview, as these are best discussed in a later stage.

WRITE YOUR SAMPLE RESPONSE HERE:

_____
_____
_____
_____

BE PERSISTENT

If you're having trouble finding a job, don't worry! There are other ways to gain skills and experience that will make you more attractive to potential employers. Consider volunteering at a local organization, starting your own small business, or participating in a school club or activity that aligns with your interests.

Remember, finding a job as a teenager is tough. It may take weeks or even months before you get hired. But don't give up. Keep applying, keep networking, and keep improving yourself. Sometimes it's just a matter of being in the right place at the right time, so don't lose hope.

ENTREPRENEURSHIP

Are you a teenager who is tired of working minimum wage jobs or babysitting for a few bucks? Have you ever thought about starting your own business? Entrepreneurship may seem like a daunting path, but it can also be one of the most rewarding experiences of your life.

The first thing you need to do is figure out if entrepreneurship is the right path for you. Starting a business requires a lot of hard work, dedication, and sacrifice. Are you willing to put in long hours, miss out on social events, and potentially lose money? If the answer is no, then entrepreneurship may not be the right path for you.

On the other hand, if you are someone who is self-motivated, enjoys taking risks, and has a passion for something specific, then starting a business may be a great option for you.

Entrepreneurship allows you to be your own boss, set your own hours, and potentially make a lot of money doing something you love.

Ask yourself the following questions if you can't decide whether starting your own business is right for you:

WHAT ARE YOUR PASSIONS?

Starting a business requires a lot of time, energy, and resources. Therefore, you need to ensure that you are passionate about the work. The drive to succeed and the desire to work hard can only come from a strong personal interest in the industry or niche of your business.

ARE YOU SELF-MOTIVATED?

Starting your own business requires an immense amount of self-motivation. You need to be willing to work tirelessly to get your business off the ground. As the boss, you are responsible for overseeing everything from accounting to marketing. Therefore, you need to have the drive to push through difficult times and most importantly, be self-disciplined.

DO YOU HAVE A SUPPORT SYSTEM?

Starting your own business requires an immense amount of self-motivation. You need to be willing to work tirelessly to get your business off the ground. As the boss, you are responsible for overseeing everything from accounting to marketing. Therefore, you need to have the drive to push through difficult times and most importantly, be self-disciplined.

DO YOU HAVE A BUSINESS PLAN?

Having a solid business plan is essential to achieving success. A business plan is written based on a deep understanding of the market, its opportunities, and its challenges. In essence, it serves as your roadmap to achieving your business goals. Therefore, you need to take the necessary time to craft an intricately detailed plan that will help you navigate the rough waters of entrepreneurship.

Starting a business requires a significant financial investment. It would be best if you had money to cover your initial expenses like a website, business license, inventory, equipment, and even salary/living expenses in the beginning stages. Thus, you need to have a detailed and realistic understanding of your finances and how you plan to finance your business.

TYPES OF BUSINESSES YOU CAN START

When it comes to starting a business, you have two options: a **not-for-profit business** or a **forprofit business**.

A not-for-profit business is a business that does not have the goal of making a profit. Instead, the goal is to provide goods or services to the community at little to no cost. For example, a not-for-profit business may be a food bank or a charity organization.	A for-profit business is a business with the goal of making a profit. For example, a for-profit business may be a clothing store, a restaurant, or a tech startup. The type of business you choose to start will depend on your goals and personal values.

Here are some other types of businesses you might pursue:

SOCIAL MEDIA MANAGEMENT

With the rise of the internet and social media platforms, social media management is a growing field that provides a host of opportunities for teens looking to start their own businesses. If you have experience in managing social media accounts and creating content, offering your services as a social media manager to small businesses or influencers could be a lucrative venture. You can charge for account creation, content creation, and even social media strategy development.

EVENT PLANNING

Do you have a passion for organizing and planning events? Event planning is an exciting business that is perfect for creative teens who love putting together parties and gatherings. Whether it's birthday parties or bridal showers, you can offer a range of event planning services such as decorations, catering, and even entertainment. Start small and work your way up as you gain experience.

TUTORING AND COACHING:

If you excel in a particular subject or have a talent that you're passionate about, offering coaching and tutoring services is a great way to share your knowledge and skills with others. You could offer tutoring services for school subjects, music lessons, or even coach individuals in sports, arts, o public speaking. As a tutor or coach, you can set your own rates and choose your own clients.

BLOGGING AND CONTENT CREATION:

If writing is your passion, blogging and content creation may be the perfect business for you. Starting a blog or YouTube channel is a great way to share your ideas and insights with others, while also generating income through advertising or sponsorships. With the rise of influencer marketing, creators with a niche following can even receive free products or paid partnerships with their favorite brands.

ONLINE RESELLING:

Online reselling on platforms like eBay, Amazon or Poshmark is a great business idea for teens who are interested in fashion and shopping. You can buy high-quality items for a lower price and then resell them for a profit. You can also source items from family or friends' closets and thrift stores to sell. As you gain more experience, you could even expand into wholesale or drop shipping.

GENERAL TIPS FOR STARTING YOUR OWN BUSINESS

If you are ready to start your own business, here are a few tips to help you along the way:

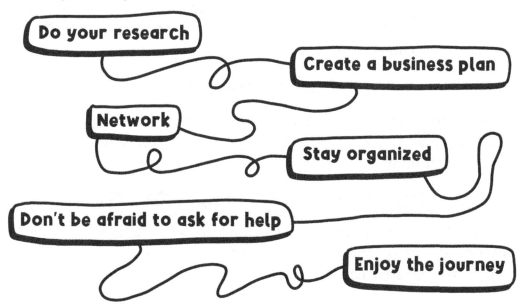

Do your research

Create a business plan

Network

Stay organized

Don't be afraid to ask for help

Enjoy the journey

DO YOUR RESEARCH

Before starting a business, make sure you research your industry, your competition, and your target market. This will help you to make informed decisions and set achievable goals.

CREATE A BUSINESS PLAN

A business plan is a roadmap for your business. It should outline your goals, objectives, target market, financials, and overall strategy. Creating a business plan will not only help you stay organized, but it will also make it easier to secure funding, find investors, and partners. A well-crafted business plan is essential for anyone starting a business.

NETWORK

t's important to network and make connections with other professionals in your industry. This can help you to find new customers, investors, and mentors. Finding a mentor who can guide you through the process of starting and growing a business can be invaluable. They can help you avoid common mistakes, provide much-needed advice, and help you navigate the business world.

STAY ORGANIZED

As a teenage entrepreneur, you will have a lot on your plate. Make sure to stay organized by keeping a schedule, setting goals, and documenting important information.

DON'T BE AFRAID TO ASK FOR HELP

Starting a business can be overwhelming. Don't be afraid to ask for help from friends, family, or local resources such as your chamber of commerce or small business center.

ENJOY THE JOURNEY

Starting a business is an exciting and rewarding experience. Take time to enjoy the journey and celebrate your successes along the way.

Chapter 12: Money Makes the World Go 'Round

Growing up, I never really paid much attention to money management. I spent most of my allowance on clothes, movies, and unnecessary items. But then, when I was in college and living on my own, I realized how important it was to make my money work for me. I learned the hard way that good money management is essential for teens, and here's why.

When you start managing your own money, you gain a sense of responsibility that will benefit you throughout your life. If you learn the basics of money management as a teen, you'll be well-equipped to handle your finances as you get older and start making larger purchases.

This will help you to make decisions that are in your financial best interest, rather than just those that seem fun at the time.

Whether it's learning to save, budget, or invest, taking control of your finances now can lead to a brighter financial future down the road.

Let's take a closer look at how you can make your money work for you.

MONEY MANAGEMENT

Being a teenager can be tough, and it can become even harder if you are not careful with your money. That's why it's crucial to start learning good money management skills right from the start.

First and foremost, it's essential to know what you want to achieve with your money. Whether it's saving up for a new car, paying for college, or buying that new gadget, setting specific financial goals can guide your spending decisions.

Once you have identified your goals, you can create a budget that will help you achieve them.

WRITE DOWN YOUR FINANCIAL GOALS BELOW:

_____

_____

_____

_____

_____

_____

BUDGETING

Budgeting may seem like a drag, but it's a necessary skill to learn no matter what age you are. But it's important to develop good habits early on. By budgeting wisely, you can avoid financial stress, save up for the things you want, and set yourself up for a successful financial future.

Once you have your goals in mind, it's time to start tracking your income and expenses. This means keeping track of your money coming in (allowance, part-time job, etc.) and your money going out (lunch money, clothes, entertainment, etc.).

There are plenty of apps and tools out there to help you with this, or you can simply use a spreadsheet or notebook. The important thing is to be consistent and keep track of everything.

Here are some apps to try:

Greenlight   Quicken   MoneyFit

Mint   Tip Yourself   Bankaroo

Now that you know where your money is going, it's time to create a budget. This means setting limits on your spending and making sure that you're not overspending in any one category.

The 50/30/20 rule is a good place to start:

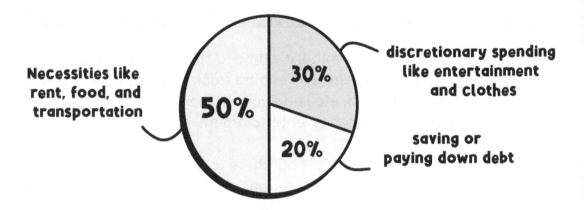

Necessities like rent, food, and transportation — 50%

discretionary spending like entertainment and clothes — 30%

saving or paying down debt — 20%

It's easy to get caught up in the moment and make impulsive purchases, but these can quicklyderail your budget. Before you buy anything, take a step back and ask yourself if it's something you really need or if you can afford it.

Don't be afraid to give yourself some time to think about it before making a decision. And always keep your financial goals in mind: will this purchase help you get closer to them, or will it take you further away?

Gamechanger:
Remember that budgeting is not a fixed science. Your income and expenses may vary from month to month, and you may need to adjust your budget accordingly. Don't beat yourself up if you go over budget one month – just look for ways to make it up next month. And don't forget to celebrate your successes along the way!

BUDGET CREATION ACTIVITY

Here's an activity to try.

STEP 1: LIST YOUR EXPENSES

The first step in budgeting is to start by listing out all your expenses. Include everything that you spend money on, including snacks, clothing, entertainment, and other miscellaneous items. This step is an eye-opener when you see how small expenses can add up quickly.

_____

_____

_____

_____

_____

_____

STEP 2: DETERMINE YOUR INCOME

After listing your expenses, it is essential to determine your income. If you have a regular paycheck, this step is easy, but if you earn money from odd jobs, babysitting, or other means, try to estimate your income. It is essential to be realistic about your income, so you don't overestimate and end up with a budget deficit.

_____

_____

_____

_____

_____

_____

STEP 3: DiVIDE YOUR EXPENSES INTO CATEGORIES

Once you have listed all expenses, divide them into categories such as transportation, food, entertainment, and clothing. This step helps you identify where most of your money goes. You may realize that you spend way too much on clothing, which is an area where you can cut back to save money.

_____
_____
_____
_____
_____

STEP 4: SET A BUDGET

Based on your expenses and income, set a budget for each category. Allocate money that you will spend in each category for the month. For instance, you can allocate $50 for entertainment, $100 for food, and $50 for transportation. It is essential to stay within the budget and avoid overspending.

_____
_____
_____
_____
_____

STEP 5: TRACK YOUR EXPENSES

To ensure that you stick to your budget, track all your expenses. When you buy something, write it down and subtract it from the allocated budget. This step can be tedious, but it helps identify where you are overspending and where you can reduce your expenses.

_____
_____
_____
_____
_____

CREDIT

Credit is one of the most important things you need to grasp early on. Knowing what credit is and how it works can save you from future financial mistakes.

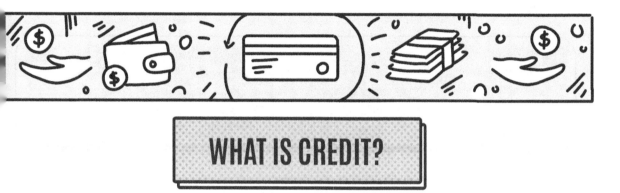

WHAT IS CREDIT?

Credit is the ability to borrow money to purchase goods or services. It's like an IOU that you must pay back at a later date with interest. Credit can be extremely beneficial when used wisely.

For example, you can use credit to buy a car or finance your education. However, irresponsible use of credit can negatively affect your financial future.

HOW DOES CREDIT SCORE WORK?

Credit score is a number that creditors (lenders) use to determine your ability to pay back loans. It ranges from 350 to 850, with higher scores indicating higher ability to pay back loans. Your credit score is calculated based on several factors, including payment history, credit utilization, length of credit history, and credit mix.

Paying your bills on time and utilizing credit wisely can raise your credit score, while late payments, high credit utilization, and opening several new credit accounts in a short period can lower it.

WHY IS CREDIT IMPORTANT?

Credit is essential for a variety of reasons. It's necessary to make purchases for things like a car or a home. Your credit history can also impact your ability to rent an apartment, apply for a job, or secure a loan.

GameChanger:
Building good credit takes time and starting early is important because the longer you have a record of responsible credit use, the better it is for your credit score.

HOW CAN YOU BUILD CREDIT?

As a teenager, you may not have a long credit history, but there are several ways to start building credit.

One way is to become an authorized user on a parent or guardian's credit card. This allows you to make small purchases under their account, and their timely payments will reflect positively on your credit history.

Another way is to open a secured credit card. A secured credit card requires a security deposit and typically has a low credit limit but can be an effective method for building credit.

CREDIT TIPS

From leasing an apartment to owning a car or even getting the job you want: your credit score plays a vital role in many important financial decisions.

Opening a checking account is an excellent way to start building your credit history.

Gamechanger:
Some banks offer "teen checking accounts," which can help you establish a credit profile. Be sure to use the account responsibly, including depositing your allowance and birthday gift checks, and paying bills on time.

Borrowing money through credit cards is a huge responsibility. However, if you use your cards responsibly, it can help you establish good credit habits. For instance, you can consider getting a secured credit card, which you put a certain amount of money in as collateral. It can limit the amount you can borrow and make it easier to control spending.

If your parents have good credit history, you can request that they add you as an authorized user to their credit accounts. Their credit activity will reflect on your credit history as well.

Making payments on time is one of the most effective ways to boost your credit score. Whether it's your phone bill or car insurance, it's essential to make timely payments. Late payments have a significant impact on your credit score and show financial irresponsibility. It is best to pay off the balance in full monthly to avoid accruing interest.

SAVING

While it may seem like a far-off concept, saving money is an essential part of building a secure life. One great way to start saving is by opening a savings account. Not only does this provide a secure place to keep your money, but it can also earn you interest to help your savings grow.

To open a savings account, you typically need to be at least 13 years old. Some banks may have specific age requirements, so it's essential to check with your local bank to see what their rules are. You may need to have a parent or guardian co-signer on the account if you are under 18 years old.

Most savings accounts do not have monthly maintenance fees, and many allow you to make unlimited withdrawals without penalty. However, some banks may charge fees for specific account types or for using non-network ATMs. Make sure to read the terms and conditions of any account you are considering carefully.

> **Gamechanger:**
> Most banks allow you to make deposits through direct deposit, ATM deposits, or in-person at a branch location. Withdrawals can typically be made through ATM withdrawals or in-person at a branch location. Some banks may also offer mobile banking options, which allow you to deposit and withdraw money through their mobile app.

INTEREST RATES

Interest rates can vary depending on the bank and account type, but typically range from 0.01% to 1% APY (Annual Percentage Yield).

While these may seem like small numbers, remember that any interest earned is extra money that you didn't have before. Additionally, some banks offer higher interest rates for higher account balances, so it's essential to compare options and find an account that fits your needs.

WHAT TO LOOK FOR IN A SAVINGS ACCOUNT

When choosing a savings account, it's important to consider several factors. Some things to look for include:

- ⊕ No monthly maintenance fees
- ⊕ No minimum balance requirements
- ⊕ Competitive interest rates
- ⊕ Accessibility to ATMs and branch locations
- ⊕ Mobile banking options

MORE SAVINGS TIPS FOR TEENS

Aside from putting money in a savings account, there are a few other tips you can follow to save some money:

Save Money Automatically

Many banks now offer automatic savings options that will help you save money without even noticing it. When you receive your allowance, have a portion of it automatically transferred to your savings account. This will help you build up your savings over time, and you won't even have to think about it.

Use Coupons and Discount Codes:

Whether you're shopping online or in stores, always be on the lookout for coupons and discount codes. You'd be surprised at how much you can save by spending a few minutes searching for promo codes. There are also many apps like Honey that automatically find and apply codes to your purchases, saving you money without any extra effort.

Learn to Say "No"

Peer pressure can be a big factor in overspending. Just because your friends are spending money on certain things doesn't mean you have to do the same. Learn to say "no" to unnecessary purchases and activities and only spend money on things that are important to you.

Make Your Own Meals

Eating out can be expensive, especially if you're doing it frequently. Instead, try making your own meals at home. Not only will you save money, but you'll also learn how to cook, which is a valuable life skill. You can even make meal prep a fun social activity with your friends.

FINANCIAL AID

As a teenager, you may think that financial aid is only for college students or adults who are struggling to make ends meet. However, there are plenty of financial assistance programs available to help teens cover the costs of education, extracurricular activities, and more.

SCHOLARSHIPS AND GRANTS

Scholarships and grants are perhaps the most well-known forms of financial aid. Scholarships are typically awarded based on academic, athletic, or artistic achievement, while grants are usually based on need.

You can start your search for scholarships and grants by checking with your school counselor or searching online. Countless opportunities are available, and you may be surprised at what you can qualify for.

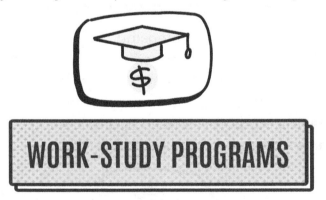

WORK-STUDY PROGRAMS

Work-study programs allow you to earn money to help pay for college or other expenses. These programs are typically offered through colleges and universities and provide part-time jobs for students, often on campus. The pay can vary, but it's a great opportunity to gain work experience while earning some money to help pay for your education.

YOUTH PROGRAMS AND SERVICES

Many organizations offer programs and services specifically for young people, which can include financial assistance. For example, the Boys and Girls Clubs of America offer scholarships and other forms of assistance to members who need it. If you're involved in any organizations or programs, be sure to ask if they offer any financial aid options.

CROWDFUNDING

Crowdfunding is becoming an increasingly popular way to raise money for a variety of causes, including education expenses. There are many online platforms available, such as GoFundMe, that allow you to create a fundraising campaign and share it with your network. This can be a great way to get the support you need to afford things like study abroad programs or expensive sports equipment.

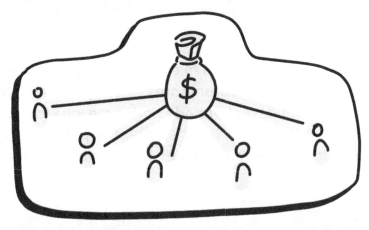

THE FAFSA

The FAFSA is a free program that helps students pay for college. It applies to both undergraduate and graduate students. Any student who is a U.S. citizen or an eligible non-citizen and is attending an eligible post-secondary school can apply for the FAFSA.

The program offers government-based financial aid such as Pell Grants, Federal Work-Study Programs, Direct Loans, and others.

The FAFSA application is accessible online, and you can start applying in October of the year before the academic year you're applying for. Here are a few steps to follow to apply for the FAFSA.

☐ **Gather Required Documents**: Before applying, collect identification documents such as social security card, driver's license, and tax returns while ensuring you have access to the internet.

☐ **Create an FSA ID**: Obtain an FSA ID for you and one for your parents or guardians who would be offering that necessary information. This ID allows you to sign and complete your application.

☐ **Fill Out the FAFSA Form**: Using your FSA ID, fill out the application form online accurately. Include your financial details like the tax returns for both students and parents to determine eligibility.

☐ **Submit**: Make sure you have double-checked and submitted your application. And select the schools you want to receive your application.

OTHER WAYS TO APPLY FOR FINANCIAL AID

FAFSA is not the only option for financial aid. Other private organizations and scholarships can offer funding assistance. Other sources of funding include:

Review Institutional Grants: The college you opt for may offer financial aid in addition to the FAFSA application. Apply for it to qualify for additional funds.

Check for Private Scholarships: Private organizations come up with their scholarships to support students. Check the internet or inquire about the institution you want to join.

Look Out for Nonprofits: Organizations and foundations aim to provide aid to low income communities' students to pursue their education.

Submit the CSS Profile: Submit the CSS Profile, a financial aid application used by colleges, universities, and scholarships to understand your financial needs.

DEADLINES

Deadlines are important to meet when applying for financial aid. Here are a few deadlines to write down:

- **FAFSA deadline:** Federal deadlines for submitting FAFSA for the upcoming academic year are June 30th.

- **State Deadlines:** In certain states, there are specific deadlines to follow to be eligible for State Aid. Check your state's deadline to avoid last-minute submissions.

- **Institution Deadlines:** Each college has its deadlines. Be sure to submit your FAFSA andother aid applications before their specific dates.

STUDENT LOANS

Student loans are a type of financial aid that helps students pay for higher education. With student loans, you borrow money from a lender - typically the federal government or a private financial institution - to pay for tuition, room and board, textbooks, and other related expenses.

While student loans should be a last resort, they can be a helpful tool in financing your education. Be sure to research your options and understand the terms and interest rates before taking out any loans.

Gamechanger:
Remember that you will be responsible for paying these loans back after graduation, so borrow only what you need and have a plan for repayment.

There are two types of student loans:

Federal Loans:
These loans are funded by the government and are available to students who complete the FAFSA. There are two types of federal loans: subsidized and unsubsidized. Subsidized student loans are based on financial need, while unsubsidized loans are not.

Private Loans:
These loans are not funded by the government and are available from banks and credit unions. Interest rates and terms can vary depending on the lender, and most private loans will require a credit check or a qualified co-signer.

Before choosing a student loan, it is important to understand your options and the terms and conditions of each option. You should also consider the total cost of borrowing over the life of the loan, including interest rates, fees, and repayment terms. Ideally, you want to choose a loan that offers a low-interest rate, flexible repayment options, and manageable monthly payments.

Whether you choose a federal or private student loan, you will be responsible for repaying the borrowed amount, plus any interest and fees. Repayment typically begins after a grace period, which is usually six months after graduation.

The terms of repayment can vary, depending on the type of loan and the lender, but most offer the option to pay over 10-25 years.

Now that you know these tips, let's take a look at some helpful strategies for paying your bills as an adult.

Chapter 13: Paying Your Bills

Let's be honest, paying bills is probably the last thing any of us wants to do. However, once we hit a certain age, it becomes an inevitable responsibility that we cannot ignore. Trust me, I learned this the hard way.

As a teenager, I couldn't care less about my bills, and I was oblivious to the negative impacts of not paying them on time. However, now that I'm older, wiser, and have a bit more experience, I'd love to share a story with you.

It all started when I was in college. I had just received my first credit card, and I was thrilled to have financial independence. Unfortunately, my excitement led me to make some mistakes.

One day, I received my credit card bill, and to my surprise, I had exceeded my credit limit. Instead of paying the minimum amount, I decided to pay only half of it and save the rest for later. It seemed like a good idea at the time, and I thought I'd have plenty of time to pay it off.

Fast forward several months later, and my credit card had accumulated high-interest rates, and I had missed several payments. I was in deep trouble, and I didn't know how to get out of it. I realized that paying bills on time is not just a responsibility but an essential part of keeping your finances stable.

Let's learn more about exactly how to do that.

ONLINE VERSUS IN PERSON

As we venture further into adulthood, one of the essential responsibilities we'll face is paying our bills. And while some of us may resort to online payments, others still prefer doing it the "old-fashioned" way, which is through in-person transactions.

Let's weigh some of the pros and cons.

PROS OF ONLINE PAYMENT

Convenience: Paying bills online is arguably the most popular option among millennials, thanks to its unparalleled convenience. You can pay your bills from anywhere, anytime – all you need is your smartphone, tablet, or laptop with a stable internet connection.

Time efficiency: Since online payment works 24/7, you can schedule and automate your payments in just a few clicks. This feature is particularly helpful for forgetful individuals as it eliminates the possibility of late payments or missed deadlines.

CONS OF ONLINE PAYMENT

➤ **Technical difficulties**: The only downside to online payments is when unforeseen technical issues prevent you from making transactions. These issues may include network outages, system crashes, or even virus attacks.

➤ **Security risks**: Despite advancements in online payment security protocols, the risk of hackers stealing your personal and financial information always looms. One of the most effective ways to minimize these risks is to ensure that you pay your bills only on trusted payment platforms.

PROS & CONS OF IN-PERSON PAYMENT

PROs

Human interaction: One of the biggest advantages of doing in-person payments is that it allows you to interact with people who might be able to guide you through the payment process. Plus, you can raise any concerns about the service and ask questions about the payment policies.

Credibility: Paying your bills in person can also give the impression that you are a credible and trustworthy individual. This perception can be particularly advantageous when filing for loans or opening new accounts, as it shows that you are dependable when it comes to financial matters.

CONs

Time consuming: In today's fast-paced world, time is precious. Waiting in line to pay your bills can be frustrating and time-consuming, which can be a challenge, particularly for people who have a hectic schedule.

Location: Accessibility is another drawback of the in-person payment method. Not all payment centers are conveniently located, making it hard for you to make your payments on time.

PAYING ON TIME

Bills are a part of adulthood, but for teenagers just starting to handle their finances, it can be overwhelming. Paying bills on time is important to keep credit scores high and avoid late fees.

☐ SET A BUDGET

Again, the first step to paying your bills on time is to create a budget. List all your monthly expenses, including bills, subscriptions, and any other recurring expenses you may have. Once you have identified all of these expenses, compare it to your monthly income. If your expenses exceed your income, you need to make some cuts. You can either reduce expenses or increase your income.

☐ SET UP AUTOMATIC PAYMENTS

Setting up automatic billing is the easiest way to ensure that you never miss a payment. Most companies offer this service, and it's usually free. You just have to provide your bank account details or credit card information, and they will automatically deduct the payment on a specific date each month. If you're afraid of overdrafts, check with your bank about setting up overdraft protection.

☐ CREATE A REMINDER SYSTEM

If you prefer to do things manually, you can use a reminder system. You can set reminders on your phone or computer to alert you when your bills are due. Alternatively, you can use a calendar or planner to keep track of your payment due dates. Make sure to set the alert a few days in advance so you can ensure that you have the funds available to make the payment.

☐ MAKE PARTIAL PAYMENTS

If you're having trouble making a payment in full, you can make partial payments to help reduce the burden. Most companies will accept partial payments, although they may charge late fees for payments that aren't paid in full. Just make sure to communicate with the company and let them know that you're making partial payments.

☐ DON'T IGNORE YOUR BILLS

Ignoring your bills won't make them go away. In fact, ignoring your bills can lead to late fees, interest charges, and eventually, collections. If you're having trouble making a payment, contact the company and try to work out a payment plan. Most companies are willing to work with you as long as you communicate with them.

LATE PAYMENTS

We've all been there - those moments where we forget to pay a bill on time or just simply can't afford to. Late payments can have a huge impact on your finances, affecting your credit score, interest rates, and even your ability to rent an apartment or get a loan.

Late payments are simply payments made after the due date. While it may not seem like a big deal, even one late payment can have a significant impact on your credit score. Late payments are typically reported to credit bureaus around 30 days after the due date and can stay on your credit report for up to seven years.

Not only can this affect your ability to get approved for credit, it can also lead to higher interest rates and fees.

Of course, one of the simplest ways to avoid late payments is to keep track of your due dates. Write them down on a calendar or set up reminders on your phone or computer. This way, you'll never forget when a bill is due and can avoid late fees and penalties.

Use the calendar below to help you keep track of your bill due dates:

Calendar

Sun	Mon	Tue	Wed	Thu	Fri	Sat
	1	2	3	4	5	6
7	8	9	10	11	12	13
14	15	16	17	18	19	20
21	22	23	24	25	26	27
28	29	30	31			

LATE FEES

Picture this: you're just starting to establish credit in and you get a bill for something you used a few months ago, and suddenly there's an extra charge labeled "late fee." What does that even mean? Why are you getting charged for something that's already past due?
And what can you do to avoid it from happening again?

First things first: what are late fees? Late fees are additional charges that are added to your bill if you fail to pay it by the due date. Basically, if you miss the deadline for payment, you'll likely get hit with a fee. These fees can vary depending on the company, and they can add up quickly if you continue to miss payments.

So, why should you care about late fees? For one, they can seriously damage your credit score. If you continuously miss payments and accrue late fees, it sends a bad signal to lenders and creditors about your ability to pay back debts. This can make it more difficult for you to get approved for loans or lines of credit in the future, or you may be offered higher interest rates as a result.

Late fees can also be a total waste of money. They're essentially a penalty for not being responsible with your payments, and they can eat away at your budget over time. For example, let's say you have a credit card bill for $100 with a late fee of $25. If you continue to miss payments every month and accrue a late fee each time, you'll end up spending an extra $300 over the course of a year. That's money you could've spent on something way more fun and worthwhile!

Gamechanger:
The easiest and most effective way to avoid late fees is to simply pay your bills on time. Sounds simple enough, but it's not always easy to remember when you're juggling multiple bills and due dates. One strategy is to set up automatic payments through your bank account or use a budgeting app that sends reminders when bills are due.

Another option is to negotiate with the company if you're having trouble making payments. Reach out to customer service and explain your situation - they may be willing to offer a payment plan or waive the late fee as a one-time courtesy. However, this isn't something you'll want to rely on every month, as it can be much more difficult to get late fees waived if you're a repeat offender.

EFFECTS OF CREDIT

First, let's start with a basic definition of credit: it's when you borrow money with the promise to pay it back in a certain period of time.

Credit can be acquired through various means, such as a credit card or loan.

Now, what are the effects of credit on your wallet? One of the biggest impacts is on your credit score. A credit score is a number that lenders use to determine how reliable you are as a borrower. The higher the score, the better the chance you'll have of being approved for things like loans or credit cards with better terms and interest rates.

However, if you miss a payment or default on a loan, this can negatively affect your credit score. A poor credit score can lead to higher interest rates and difficulty in being approved for credit. This is why it's important to make your payments on time and keep your credit balances low.

Another effect of credit on your wallet is the interest rate that you will be charged for borrowing money.

Gamechanger:
Interest rates vary depending on the type of credit you're using, but the higher the interest rate, the more money you'll have to pay back in addition to what you've borrowed. This is why it's important to shop around for the best interest rates before committing to borrowing money.

Credit can also impact your spending habits. It's easy to get caught up in the excitement of having a credit card and overspend; leading to debt that can quickly spiral out of control. It's important to use credit responsibly and within your means. That means using your credit card for small purchases and paying off the balance in full each month.

Lastly, credit can impact your future financial goals, such as buying a car or a house. Lenders will look at your credit score and history when deciding whether to approve you for a loan. A good credit score and history can lead to better loan terms and a better chance of being approved for the loan you need.

BELOW, WRITE YOUR ANSWER TO THIS QUESTION: WHY DO YOU WANT GOOD CREDIT?

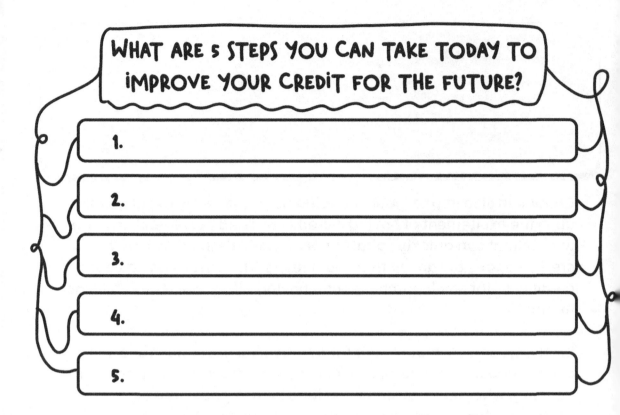

WHAT ARE 5 STEPS YOU CAN TAKE TODAY TO IMPROVE YOUR CREDIT FOR THE FUTURE?

1.

2.

3.

4.

5.

And what's one reason you might need a loan? To buy a car! In the next chapter, we'll take a closer look at what goes into car ownership and maintenance.

Chapter 14:
Car Ownership

I remember the first time I set my eyes on my first car – it was love at first sight. The excitement that came with the prospect of finally owning a car was overwhelming, but so was the stress that came with it.

Before I made up my mind to buy my first car, I spent weeks researching and scrutinizing every option available to me. I talked to friends and family, read reviews, and even went as far as conducting online surveys to determine which car would serve my needs best. I finally settled on a used car that I found on a popular car dealership website.

As soon as I saw the car in person, I felt like it was the perfect fit for me. It was not a perfect car, but every scratch and ding just made it feel more unique. I spent hours negotiating the price with the salesman before eventually agreeing to a deal. The whole process was mentally draining.

After the deal was sealed, the paperwork started. Signing countless reams of paper and very long contracts made me realize that there was so much more to owning a car than driving it. The excitement that once filled me was slowly being replaced by the realization of the responsibilities involved with owning a car.

Paying for insurance, gas, maintenance, and registration was all new to me. As a teenager who was used to relying on my parents to take care of my needs, this was a massive shift in responsibility that up until that moment, I had not understood fully. As the days went by, the stress began to dissipate, and the excitement returned.

Driving my first car was an incredible experience. I felt like I had gained a new kind of freedom. The car was mine, and I could drive it wherever I wanted, whenever I wanted. The joy of independence was unmatched, and it was then that I realized that all the stress and hassle had been worth it.

It's no secret that buying a car, especially for the first time, can be a daunting experience. Let's break things down a bit more.

WHAT ARE YOU LOOKING FOR IN YOUR FIRST CAR? WHAT MAJOR CHARACTERISTICS ARE IMPORTANT TO YOU? WRITE THEM DOWN BELOW AND BRING THIS LIST WITH YOU WHEN YOU FIRST START CAR SHOPPING.

- ☐ _____
- ☐ _____
- ☐ _____
- ☐ _____
- ☐ _____
- ☐ _____

LEASING

As a teen, you might be itching to get behind the wheel and cruise around town in your own car. However, buying a car may not be the best option for you right now. That's where leasing comes in. Leasing a car is a great option for many young drivers, but it can be tricky to understand all the ins and outs.

Simply put, leasing a car is like renting a car, but for a longer period, usually 2 to 5 years. When you lease a car, you pay a monthly fee for the use of the car, just like you would with renting an apartment. At the end of the lease agreement, you return the car to the dealership.

One of the biggest advantages of leasing a car is that you can get a newer, more expensive car for a lower monthly payment than if you were to buy the same car. This is because you're only paying for the depreciation of the car during the lease term, rather than the entire cost of the car. However, keep in mind that you won't own the car at the end of the lease term.

Another advantage of leasing is that you'll likely have lower repair and maintenance costs since the car will be under warranty during the lease period. Plus, you don't have to worry about selling the car at the end of the lease term.

When you lease a car, there are a few terms you need to understand.

First is the **"capitalized cost,"** which is the cost of the car.

Second, is the **"residual value,"** which is the estimated value of the car at the end of the lease term.

Finally, there's the **"money factor,"** which is like an interest rate on the lease. You want a low money factor to get a good deal on your lease.

Before leasing a car, make sure you understand all the terms of the lease agreement. This includes the mileage limit, any fees for excess wear and tear, and any penalties for ending the lease early. If you go over the mileage limit or cause excessive wear and tear on the car, you may be charged extra fees at the end of the lease.

PURCHASING

First things first, research is key! Before making any decisions about the car you want to buy, take some time to research. Look for the car models you like, their features, and their prices. You can read reviews from other buyers or even ask your friends about their experiences. With the internet at our fingertips, researching has never been easier.

Now that you have an idea of the prices, it's time to set a budget. Remember, a car is not just a one time purchase, but it also includes expenses like insurance, registration, and maintenance. So, make a budget that includes all these costs. It's important to be realistic and stay within your means.

Gamechanger:
There are different financing options available, like leasing or financing through the dealer or your bank. It's essential to explore all options available and compare their interest rates and terms. Don't forget to read the fine print before making any agreement.

Before making a final decision, a test drive is a must. You want to make sure the car is comfortable, safe, and suitable for your needs. Take your time and explore its features. Don't hesitate to ask the dealer or the seller any questions.

Here's a checklist of what to consider when your test driving a car:

- ☐ **Check Out the Interior**: Before you start the engine, take a look around the car to see if it has everything you need. Make sure there's enough space in the back, especially if you plan on having passengers. Test out the seats to see if they're comfortable and adjustable. Also, check out the controls and dashboard to see if they're user-friendly and easy to use while driving. If the car has any special features, make sure to test them out as well.

- ☐ **Test the Suspension**: The suspension is responsible for keeping the car smooth on the road. You should test it by driving around on a bumpy street or road. Listen for any odd noises or rattling that could signal a problem. A car that has a well-functioning suspension will make for a comfortable ride, especially on long road trips.

- ☐ **Acceleration and Braking**: The acceleration and brakes are two of the most crucial aspects of a test drive. When you accelerate, see how the car responds. Does it take too long to accelerate, or does it respond well? The same goes for braking - test how quickly the car can come to a halt in case of an emergency. You should also see how the car handles turns and sharp bends while driving.

- ☐ **Take it for a Long Drive**: Remember, this is not a joyride: this is a test. You need to test the car's capabilities under different conditions. Take it for a long drive, preferably on different types of roads - highways, neighborhoods, and side streets. This way, you can get a feel for the car in different situations. Also, take into consideration the noise level inside the car. Is it too noisy, or can you carry a conversation without raising your voice?

- ☐ **Check the Car's History**: Suppose you're considering a used car. In that case, it's essential to check the car's history before making any decisions. Ask for the car's vehicle identification number (VIN) and use a tool like Carfax to see if the car has been in any accidents or has any outstanding recalls. You should also ask for maintenance records to see if the previous owner took good care of the car.

Congratulations, you finally found your dream car! Before signing the dotted line, try negotiating the price. Make a lower offer and be confident, but always be willing to compromise. Remember, the seller or the dealer wants to sell the car as much as you want to buy it.

Can't decide whether to lease or buy? Here are some questions to ask yourself:

☐ **What is your monthly income?** – If you don't have a steady or stable income, it's a good idea to stick to a lease rather than committing to the monthly payments, obligations, and maintenance costs that come with owning a car.

☐ **How long do you want to keep your car?** – If you plan on keeping a car for a short time, say, two or three years, then leasing is the best option for you. On the other hand, if you plan on keeping your car for an extended period, owning it may be the better choice.

☐ **What is your credit score like?** – Your credit score plays a significant role in determining whether you'll be able to lease or purchase a car. While you can still lease with low credit, your financial situation will impact your monthly payment amount on both options. If you have a higher credit score, you are likely to pay less than someone with a lower rating, which could swing you towards a lease or a loan accordingly.

☐ **How important is the car's resale value to you?** – It's essential to consider the car's resale value before you even purchase it. Cars often depreciate once you drive it away from the dealership, so if you're planning on owning a car for a long time, it may be worth it to buy rather than lease.

☐ **What kind of car do you want?** – Typically, if you have your eye on a luxury car, leasing is a more affordable option than buying. The monthly payments are lower than they would be if you were to purchase the same car, and you'll have a new car to drive every few years. Additionally, buying a luxury car requires big down payments, which can be a significant barrier for teens.

WARRANTIES

So, you've finally saved enough money to buy the car you've been eyeing for months?

Congratulations! Buying a car is a huge accomplishment. But before you sign on that dotted line and drive off with your new ride, you need to know about something very important: warranties. Understanding car warranties can help you save money in the long run and make the most out of your car buying experience.

TYPES OF CAR WARRANTIES

First things first, there are different types of warranties that come with cars. The two most common types are the manufacturer's warranty and the extended warranty.

A manufacturer's warranty usually comes with a new car, and it typically covers the cost of repairs and replacements for a certain number of years or miles.

An extended warranty, on the other hand, is optional and can be bought from the car dealership or a third-party provider. This covers car repairs after the expiration of the manufacturer's warranty.

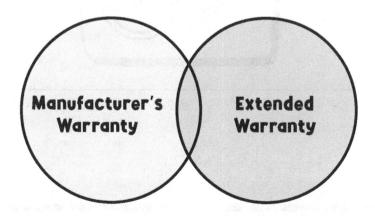

WARRANTY COVERAGE

Before you decide to purchase the car, it is important to know what exactly is covered by the warranty. Some warranties cover bumper-to-bumper repairs, while others only cover major components such as the engine or transmission.

Also, warranties have limitations and exclusions, so it is important to carefully read the warranty before signing any contracts to know what exactly is covered and what areas may be excluded.

WARRANTY PERIOD

Another crucial factor to consider is the duration of the warranty. The warranty period varies by manufacturer and model, and it can range anywhere from one to ten years. But it's also important to consider the mileage limit.

Gamechanger:
Some warranties may expire after a certain number of miles are driven, even if the period is still active, so be sure to read the fine print to know when the warranty period would end.

TRANSFERABLE WARRANTY

If you plan on selling the car soon or at some point in general, you should also consider a transferable warranty. Not all warranties are transferable, so it's important to know the details of the warranty before you purchase, in case you may decide to sell it at some point.

TRY THIS!

Use a trusted website that posts advertisements for used cars, such as auto trader. Find a car that you'd like to own, and then map out what type of investment that car will be on your finances and your time.

Print out a picture of a car you like, or draw one in the box above

CAR INFORMATION

Year/ Make / Model :

Miles/ Kilometers :

Describe the Condition of the Car :

Is there a warranty?

Research the Fuel Efficiency
[Tip: if it doesn't tell you on the
listing, then google
the Fuel Efficiency of the year,
make and model of the car.]

FINANCIALS

What would the monthly payments be?

What is the interest rate?

How much would the insurance be?

THE TOTALS

How much money does this car cost per month?

How much of your monthly budget can you spend on this car?

Do you think buying this car is a wise financial decision?

MAINTENANCE

Owning a car is one of the biggest milestones and an exciting time in your life. The freedom and independence it gives you can be liberating, but it also comes with responsibilities, including car maintenance. Proper car maintenance is crucial to keep your vehicle in excellent shape and prevent costly damages in the future.

Here are a few key items to tend to:

- ☐ **Regular changing of oil, oil filter, and air filter** – these three are the essential components of the vehicle's engine. Changing the oil and oil filter ensures that the engine is lubricated and cleaned out of buildup, while the air filter ensures that the engine is getting clean air. We recommend changing your oil and oil filter every 5,000 to 7,500 miles and your air filter every 12,000 miles.

- ☐ **Maintain your battery** – the battery is the heart of your car's electrical system. Ensure that it's clean, connected correctly, and not leaking. Test your battery regularly and replace it every three to five years.

- ☐ **Check tires' air pressure and rotate them regularly** – tire pressure plays a significant role in car safety and fuel efficiency. Check your tire pressure every month and rotate your tires every six months to ensure even wear.

- ☐ **Regular brake maintenance** – brake safety is critical for your safety and other road users. Ensure that your brake pads, rotors, and brake fluid are in good condition by having them inspected twice a year.

- ☐ **Keep your car clean** – Keeping your car clean inside and outside not only makes it look good but helps to prevent corrosion and scratches on your vehicle's paint. Clean your car by washing it every two weeks, and use car wax to keep your car's paint shining.

HOW TO CHANGE A TIRE ON A CAR

| Loosen Lug nuts | Jack Up the Car | Change the Tire | Tighten the Nuts |

HOW TO CHANGE THE OIL IN A CAR

| Drain the oil | Replace the Filter | Replace the Drain Plug | Add new Oil |

As you research different cars, think about the kind of driving experience you would like - practical or stylish, luxury or compact. Start the process by getting an idea of the type of car that fits all your must-haves, and start saving!

To wrap up this post, why not draw your dream car below? Who knows - maybe one day you'll be able to make it a reality!

Next, we'll explore how to find the right type of housing as a teen. After all, a car is important, but you also need somewhere to sleep!

Chapter 15:
Housing

When I was a teenager, all I wanted was to have a place of my own, away from my parents' prying eyes. I remember scrolling through housing ads on Craigslist and feeling overwhelmed by the amount of information there was to sift through. The process of finding my first apartment was daunting, but it was also one of the most exhilarating experiences of my life.

I'll walk you through some tips to help make the process easier for you.

APARTMENT RENTAL

As a teenager, it's normal to long for independence and freedom. One way to start experiencing it is by renting an apartment. However, it's also a huge responsibility that comes with numerous decisions that can be overwhelming for anyone, let alone for someone who is just going out on their own.

Before you dive into the rental market, do your research. Start by finding the ideal location, then research the average cost of rent in the area, the amenities included with rentals, and what you can afford on your budget. You can check online portals like Craigslist, Zillow, or Apartments.com for rental listings that fit your criteria.

TIPS FOR FINDING AN APARTMENT

Before you start looking for apartments, it's important to figure out how much you can afford to spend each month. Make a list of all your expenses, including rent, utilities, groceries, transportation, and leisure activities. Then, subtract that total from your income. This will give you an idea of your discretionary income, which you can use to rent an apartment. As a general rule, your rent should not exceed 30% of your net income.

Next, consider your must-haves. Ask yourself the following questions:

☐ Do I need to be close to public transportation?

☐ Do I want a pet-friendly building?

☐ How far away from family, friends, or my job can I be?

☐ Do I mind sharing with another person or family?

☐ Do I need a certain number of bedrooms or bathrooms?

Think about what you need to feel comfortable in your home and prioritize those things in your search.

LOOK FOR ROOMMATES

Renting an apartment with roommates can be a great way to save money and build friendships. If you have friends who are also looking for housing, consider renting a place together.

If you don't have any potential roommates, look for ads in your local college or community center. You can also use websites like Roomster or Craigslist to find compatible roommates.

DON'T BE AFRAID TO NEGOTIATE

Once you find an apartment that you like, don't be afraid to negotiate with the landlord. Ask if they would be willing to lower the monthly rent or offer you a discount for signing a longer lease.

Be confident in your ability to find another apartment if the negotiations don't work out. There are always other options out there.

WATCH FOR RED FLAGS

One of the most significant decisions when you start searching for your first apartment is choosing a landlord. Your landlord holds much of the responsibility for your comfort, safety, and security in your new home. Keep an eye out for these red flags to know if a landlord is someone you can trust.

Poor Communication: One of the most evident red flags in a landlord is their communication. If they are not responding to your messages or calls, or they only reply after a long while, that's a sign that they may not be easy to reach in case of an emergency. It could also mean that they may not be prioritizing your needs as a tenant.

Pushy Promises: If a landlord ensures you that they will fix any damages, provide amenities or upgrades that delight you, or come with a 'too good to be true' offer, you should be wary. Before signing a lease or handing over any money, ensure those promises are listed in the lease agreement or get them in writing

Unkempt/Dirty Property: The property's condition can say a lot about how invested the landlord is in his or her properties. If the common areas or apartments are unkempt, smelly, or in disrepair, it's a big red flag. Leaky faucets, moldy walls, or malfunctioning appliances, besides being major inconveniences for you, can indicate that the landlord is not taking a proactive approach to property maintenance.

No Screening Process: If the landlord does not ask for a background check, rental history, or references, that's a red flag. It's important to understand that while they may not be legally required to screen tenants, it's a standard practice for any professional landlord. This process ensures the landlord attracts tenants who will pay rent on time and ensure they're letting decent people onto their property.

High Pressure: If the landlord pushes you to sign the lease quickly or requests you pay a large sum of money upfront to secure the apartment, take caution. Rushing you into signing the lease can mean that the landlord does not want you to read it carefully or consult with a lawyer. Remember that a signed lease is legally binding, so take your time to review it and ensure you understand all of its terms.

READ THE LEASE CAREFULLY

Before signing a lease, make sure you read it carefully. You should understand all the terms and conditions of the agreement before committing to it. Here are a few things to pay attention to:

Rent and Fees:
Your lease should clearly outline the amount of rent and any fees you are required to pay, as well as the due dates. Make sure you understand how much you owe and when it's due. Also, keep an eye out for any late fees, returned check fees, or other charges that may be hidden in the fine print.

Duration of the Lease:
How long will your lease last? Make sure you know when the lease starts and ends and if it will automatically renew. If it does, you'll want to know how much notice you need to give if you plan on moving out. This information will help you avoid the possibility of being charged penalties for breaking the lease early.

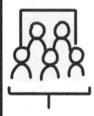

Occupancy Limits:
Your lease may specify how many people are allowed to live in the apartment, which can affect your living arrangements. If you plan on having roommates, make sure you know what your lease allows. Some leases may also prohibit subletting or Airbnb rentals, so keep this in mind if you want to rent out your apartment.

Maintenance Procedures:
Your lease should explain how to report maintenance issues and what response time you can expect. You should also know whether you are responsible for any minor repairs or maintenance tasks, such as changing light bulbs or unclogging sinks. Read through the clauses on inspections before moving out, as well as cleaning and upkeep requirements, so you don't end up losing your security deposit.

Pet Policies:
If you have a pet or plan to adopt one, make sure you understand any regulations surrounding pets. Some apartments may have breed or size limitations or require additional deposits or monthly fees. You'll want to know which areas of the complex are pet-friendly and the details of the apartment's pet rules.

Don't hesitate to ask questions or seek legal advice if you have any concerns. Remember, signing a lease is a legal and financial responsibility, so it's important to take it seriously.

CONDO/TOWNHOUSE (HOA FEES)

If you're a first-time homebuyer or just looking for a new place to call home, you've probably considered buying or renting a condo or townhouse. With their smaller size and often lower costs, these properties can be perfect for those who want to live in the city or a suburban community without breaking the bank.

WHAT IS A CONDO/TOWNHOUSE?

Let's start with the basics: What is a condo, and what is a townhouse? A condominium is a type of property where each unit is individually owned by a resident.

Common areas, such as hallways, roofs, and parking lots, are shared by all residents and maintained by the Homeowners Association, or HOA.

A townhouse, on the other hand, is a type of property that is connected to other units by shared walls. Each unit is owned by a resident and includes a yard, but the area between the houses and the roof is shared by all residents and is maintained by the HOA.

LOCATION, LOCATION, LOCATION

When it comes to buying or renting a condo or townhouse, the first thing you'll want to consider is location. Condos and townhouses can be found in a variety of communities, from urban areas to suburban neighborhoods. Consider what type of lifestyle you want and what amenities you want to be near, such as shopping, restaurants, or parks.

HOAs

Now, let's talk about HOA fees. HOA fees are monthly maintenance fees that residents pay to the Homeowners Association.

These fees will vary depending on the size and amenities of the property, but they typically cover maintenance of common areas, repairs and upgrades to the property, and other services such as security or trash removal.

> **Gamechanger:**
> HOA fees can be a significant expense, so make sure you know what you're getting into. It's important to note that HOA fees can increase over time to fund larger repairs or upgrades, such as a new roof or pool.

PRIVACY CONCERNS

Another thing to consider when buying or renting a condo or townhouse is privacy. In a condo, you will share walls and likely have neighbors living above and below you. Meanwhile, in a townhouse, you will have neighbors living next to you but may have your own entrance and outdoor space. If privacy is important to you, a townhouse may be a better fit.

BUILDING CONDITION

Finally, it's essential to consider the building's overall condition when considering a condo or townhouse. Ask to see maintenance records, inspections, and financial statements from the HOA to get a good sense of how well maintained the property is. Make sure there is a reserve fund set aside to cover any significant repairs or upgrades, such as a new roof or boilers.

HOME PURCHASING

Are you starting to think about buying a home one day? Maybe you dream of having a house with a big backyard for your dog, or maybe you want a cool loft apartment in the city! Whatever your dreams are, buying a home is a big deal, and it's important to know what you're getting into.

START WITH A BUDGET

The first thing you need to do when you're thinking about buying a home is figure out how much you can afford. This means figuring out how much money you have saved up; how much you can afford to pay for a mortgage each month, and also factoring in additional expenses like property taxes, home insurance, and maintenance costs.

Start by creating a budget and figuring out how much you can realistically afford to spend on a home.

MAKE A PUNCH LIST

When you're looking for a home, it's important to consider what your needs and wants are. Do you need a certain number of bedrooms or bathrooms? Do you want a big yard or a pool? It's important to think about what you need and what you want so that you can find a home that works for you.

_____

_____

_____

_____

_____

_____

With that said, keep in mind that it's not realistic to expect your home - especially your first home - to check off all the boxes. Keep your expectations in check!

FIND AN AGENT

Once you know your budget and your needs/wants, it's time to start looking for a real estate agent. A real estate agent can help you find the perfect home, can negotiate on your behalf, and can help guide you through the home-buying process. Make sure you choose a real estate agent that you trust and feel comfortable working with.

GET PREAPPROVED FOR A MORTGAGE

Before you start seriously looking for a home, it's a good idea to get pre-approved for a mortgage. This means that a bank or lender will evaluate your financial situation and give you a pre-approval letter that states how much money they're willing to lend you for a home. Having this pre-approval letter can help you make a stronger offer when you find a home you love.

MAKE AN OFFER AND CLOSE THE DEAL

Finally, once you find a home that you love, it's time to make an offer and close the deal! Your real estate agent will help you make an offer and negotiate with the seller to come up with a fair price.

Once the offer is accepted, you'll go through the process of getting a home inspection, signing the paperwork, and closing the deal. It can be a long and stressful process, but in the end, you'll have a home to call your own.

SUBLETTING

So you've got a lease, but you just can't stay in your apartment for the full term. Maybe you're going away for school, or perhaps you're just ready to move on to a different town or city.

Whatever the reason, subletting can be an excellent solution. It allows someone else to take over your lease for a few months, or even a year, giving you a chance to get out of an apartment you no longer want or need.

Subletting, sometimes called subleasing, is when you rent out your apartment, or a part of it, to someone else for a period of time. When you sublet your apartment, you remain the primary tenant, while the subletter becomes a temporary tenant. It's important to note that subletting is different from simply having someone stay in your apartment while you're away.

With a sublet, you're still responsible for rent payments and any damages that may occur.

Here's how to go about it.

READ LEASE AGREEMENT CAREFULLY

Before you sublet your apartment, be sure to read your lease agreement carefully. Some landlords prohibit subletting altogether, while others require that you obtain their permission first.

> **Gamechanger:**
> Many leases will include a section on subleasing that outlines what's allowed and what isn't. If you're unsure, speak to your landlord or property manager before moving forward.

ADVERTISE FOR A TENANT

Once you've confirmed that subletting is allowed in your lease, it's time to find a tenant. There are several ways to do this, including posting an ad online or asking friends and family if they know anyone who needs a place to stay.

You can also take advantage of subletting websites like Airbnb, Flipkey, or Sublet.com. These sites let you post an ad for your apartment, complete with photos and a description, and connect with potential tenants.

REVIEW TENANTS

When reviewing tenants, be sure to ask for references and check their credit scores. You also want to interview potential tenants to make sure they're a good fit.

You may want to give preference to people you know or those referred by someone you trust.

HAVE AN AGREEMENT IN PLACE

Before you hand over the keys, make sure the tenant signs a subletting agreement. This should outline the terms of the sublet, including the rent payment, security deposit, move-in and move-out dates, and any other important details.

Gamechanger:
Be sure to include the name and contact information of your landlord in case the tenant needs to get in touch with them.

STAY IN TOUCH

Once your subletter has moved in, be sure to stay in touch to ensure things are going smoothly. It's also a good idea to have a stipulation in place that allows you to inspect the apartment periodically.

Should any issues arise, handle them as soon as possible to avoid any legal complications.

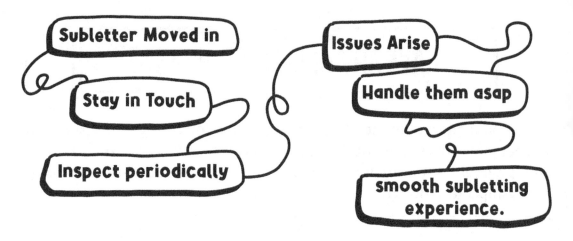

PUBLIC HOUSING

Public housing is a program designed to provide safe, decent, and affordable rental housing for low-income families, the elderly, and people with disabilities. It is owned and managed by local public housing authorities (PHAs), which are funded by the federal government.

The properties are either owned or leased by PHAs, and they are responsible for maintaining and managing the facilities. The government sets equitable rent rates to ensure that tenants pay no more than 30% of their income toward rent.

WHO is ELiGiBLE?

Generally, public housing is reserved for low-income families with limited financial resources. The eligibility criteria varies depending on the state and PHA, but generally, you must be a US citizen or a legal resident, have a household income that is below 80% of the median income of the local area, and have no history of criminal or drug-related activities. Other factors, such as family size and age, may also be considered.

Here's some more information on the HUD public housing program.

BENEFiTS OF PUBLiC HOUSiNG

Apart from the reduced rent, tenants enjoy the peace of mind that comes with knowing they have a stable and secure place to call home. They also have access to various community programs and services, such as job training, childcare, and health care, which can help them improve their quality of life.

Furthermore, public housing is often located in safe and habitable areas, providing a conducive environment for both children and adults.

Applying for Public Housing

To apply, you'll need to contact your local public housing agency, which you can find on the Department of Housing and Urban Development (HUD) website. Once you submit your application, your eligibility will be assessed, and if you're approved, you'll be placed on a waiting list.

The waiting list period can vary from a few months to a few years, depending on vacancy rates and funding. Once you're offered a unit, you'll need to sign a lease agreement, pay a security deposit, and move in. You'll also be required to re-certify your eligibility and income status annually.

ROOMMATES

Living with roommates can be a great experience. You have someone to share the rent, responsibilities, and fun times with. However, it's not always rainbows and unicorns. Sharing a living space with someone else can often lead to conflict, misunderstandings, and even hostility. So, how can you deal with roommates effectively and maintain a peaceful living space?

Here are five tips.

1. Set Clear Boundaries

Before moving in together, it's essential to have a conversation about boundaries. What are your respective expectations about cleanliness, noise level, smoking, guests, and personal space? It's crucial to establish clear rules and boundaries to prevent conflicts before they even occur. Remember to be open and honest. If you're not comfortable with something your roommate is doing, speak up calmly and respectfully. Your roommate can't read your mind, so it's better to discuss issues upfront.

2. COMMUNICATE EFFECTIVELY

Good communication is key to maintaining a healthy roommate relationship. Make sure you're expressing yourself clearly and listening to your roommate's needs as well. If there's a problem, don't let it fester. Address it as soon as possible in a diplomatic way.

Don't assume that your roommate is aware of the issue. Use "I" statements instead of blaming language.

For example, "I feel uncomfortable when you leave dishes in the sink for days" instead of "You always leave your dirty dishes everywhere."

3. DIVIDE RESPONSIBILITIES FAIRLY

Living with roommates means sharing chores and responsibilities. To avoid resentment or arguments, divide the tasks fairly based on availability, skills, and preferences. You can create a chore chart or a shared calendar to keep track of who is responsible for what.

Be respectful of your roommate's time and effort and appreciate their contributions. Don't slack off or expect your roommate to pick up after you all the time.

4. RESPECT EACH OTHER'S PRIVACY

Everyone needs some alone time or personal space, even if you're living with roommates. Respect your roommate's privacy and boundaries by knocking before entering their room, asking before borrowing their items, or letting them know in advance if you're planning to have guests over.

Avoid monopolizing common areas or making too much noise when your roommate is studying or sleeping.

5. Find Common Ground

Although you and your roommate may have different interests, values, or lifestyles, try to find some common ground to bond over.

Gamechanger:
Share stories, hobbies, music, or shows that you both enjoy. Invite your roommate to join you for a movie night, a board game, or a workout session.

Building a friendship with your roommate can make the living situation more enjoyable and less stressful. And if you ever run into difficulties, it is easier to find common ground with your roommates if you both share some of the same interests.

As teens, we are at the threshold of making life-long choices with serious consequences.

Finding the right living situation for ourselves can be a challenge - but one that is absolutely necessary to maintain our well-being and success.

Remember, when considering whether renting or buying a home is right for you, you must consider your own personal needs and circumstances. Analyze your budget, where you'd like to live, and what type of property works best for you.

Think about the institutions surrounding your possible home - is there quality transportation and education nearby? Make sure the area suits your dreams and goals before signing on any dotted lines.

Now is the time to act and go out on your own! You've got this.

Conclusion

Now that you've been given the tools to help you prepare for your next journey in life, it's time to put that knowledge into action!

THINK ABOUT EVERYTHING YOU'VE LEARNED WHILE READING THIS BOOK. THEN, MAKE A LIST OF THE TOP FIVE HABITS YOU WANT TO TRY FIRST (WRITE SOME THOUGHTS BELOW).

_____
_____
_____
_____
_____
_____

The knowledge and skills you want to acquire is likely a lengthy list – and that may be overwhelming.

But don't worry! Rome wasn't built in a day, and you don't need to master all of these life skills right away. Work slowly and steadily to become a strong, independent adult.

Remember, developing life skills is so important for your overall success in life. Don't be afraid to reach out to trusted mentors, family, and friends for advice and guidance. And if you enjoyed this book, be sure to share it with a friend.

These life skills are important for everyone, and it's never too early (or too late!) to start preparing for the road ahead.

So go ahead. Get out there and grab life by the horns. There's a big, beautiful world waiting out there for you. And now, you have the skills you need to enjoy every second of this wonderful life you've built.

WORKS CITED

D., & D. (2021, October 4)." 81% of recent college grads wish they were taught more life skills before graduation"—Published by: **digital hub US.**
Retrieved May 1, 2023 from:
 https://swnsdigital.com/us/2021/07/eighty-one- percent-of-recent-college-graduates-wish-they were taught-more-life-skills-before-graduating/

C. (n.d.)."Dental Plaque: What Is It. Causes, How to Remove. Prevent & Treat. Cleveland Clinic." Published by: **Cleveland Clinic. Org.** Retrieved May 1, 2023 from: https://my.clevelandclinic.org/health/diseases/10953-plaque
Understanding Your Skin. (n.d.). Understanding Your Skin.
https://www.en.eucerin.ca/about-skin/basic-skinknowledge/skin-types

Ultimate Guide to Feminine Hygiene Products | Duquesne University. (2023, May 18). Duquesne University School of Nursing.
https://onlinenursing.duq.edu/master-science-nursing/the-ultimate-guide-to-feminine-hygiene/

Cook, Sydney [2019] "The Ultimate Guide to Period Products." Published by: **MADE SAFE, a Program of Nontoxic Certified.** Retrieved May 1, 2023, from: https://madesafe.org/blogs/viewpoint/the-ultimate-guide-to-period-products

Goel, P. (2023, January 24). "How to T.H.1.N.K. Before You Speak and Not Put Your Foot in Your Mouth." Published by: **Orai.** Retrieved May 1, 2023, from: https://orai.com/blog/think-before-you-speak/

"Relaxation techniques: Breath control helps quell errant stress response" - Published by: **Harvard Health.** (2015, January 26). Retrieved May 1, 2023, from: https://www.health.harvard.edu/mind-and-mood/relaxation-techniques-breath-control-helps-que II-errant-stress-response

Shoemaker, M. (2019, March 21)." Try Self-Soothing Techniques When Stressed." Published in: **Jewish Exponent**. *239(49), 12.*

Ackerman, MA., C. E. (2017, March 6). 23 Amazing Health Benefits of Mindfulness for Body and Brain. Published by: **PositivePsychology.com.** Retrieved May 1, 2023, from: https://positivepsychology.com/benefits-of-mindfulness/

Thriving, E. A. (2023, January 6). "100 Positive Self Talk ExamplesTo Adopt Now - Empowered and Thriving." Published by **Empowered and Thriving.** Retrieved May 1, 2023, from: https://empoweredandthriving.com/positive-self-talk-examples/ Thriving, E. A.

(2022, April 13). "500 Positive Affirmations - Wealth, Health, More." Published by Empowered and Thriving. Retrieved May 1, 2023, from: https://empoweredandthriving.com/positive-affirmations/

(2014, December 15). "The Power of Self-Reflection: 1O Questions You Should Ask Yourself -" Published by: **LifeHack.** Retrieved May 1, 2023, from: .https://www.lifehack.org/articles/communication/the- power-self-reflection-ten-questions you-should-ask-yourself.html

Ackerman, MA., C. E. (2017, December 18). "87 Self-Reflection Questions for Introspection [+Exercises]." Published by: **PositivePsychology.com.** Retrieved May 1, 2023 https://positivepsychology.com/introspection- self-reflection/

"Sleep Loss: 10 Surprising Effects." (2014, February 13). Published by: **WebMD.** Retrieved May 1, 2023 https://www.webmd.com/sleep-disorders/features/10-results- sleep-loss

"Schools Start Too Early." (2022, October 5)—Centers for Disease Control and Prevention. Published by: **CDC**, Retrieved May 1, 2023https://www.cdc.gov/sleep/features/schools-start-too-early.html#:N:text=The%20American%20Acad emy%20of%20Pediatrics,adolescents%20start%20school%20too%20early.

Sleep for TeenagersI Sleep Foundation. (2009, April 17). Published by: **Sleep Foundation.** Retrieved May 1, 2023 https://www.sleepfoundation.org/teens-and -sleep

(2022, April 1). "Relaxation Exercises To Help Fall Asleep." Published by: **Sleep Foundation.** Retrieved May 1, 2023 https://www.sleepfoundation.org/sleep-hygiene/relaxation-exercises-to-help-fall-asleep

"Strategies to promote better sleep in these uncertain times" Published by: Harvard Health. (2020, March 27). **Harvard Health**. Retrieved May 1, 2023 https://www.health.harvard.edu/blog/strategies-to-promote-better-sleep-in-these-uncertain-time s-2020032719333

[n.d.l]. "Meditation and Mindfulness: What You Need To Know." Published by: **NCCIH.** Retrieved May 1, 2023 https://www.nccih.nih.gov/health/meditation-and-mindfulness-what-you-need-to-know

Ashbaugh, R., Schreiner, I., & Meeks, V.(2020, September 23). "6 Way to Self-Soothe When You're Feeling Triggered "- Published by: **Solid Foundations Therapy.** Retrieved May 1, 2023, https://solidfoundationstherapy.com/6-way-to-self-soothe-when-youre-feeling-triggered/

Grosso, C.(2018, April 1). "RADIATE LOVE: Cultivate a deeper sense of joy and compassion through loving-kindness meditation." Published by: **Natural Solutions**, 202, 28. Retrieved May 1, 2023

Sanford, Alafaya, Metrowest, Semoran, Kissimmee[2022, July 29]. "How much screen time per day should my child be getting? -Published by: **First Choice Pediatrics**. Retrieved May 1, 2023, https://www.fcpediatrics.com/how-much-screen-time-per-day-should-my-child-be-getting/

[n.d.l.] "Banana milk benefits: A Magical Combination for Your Health."
 Published by: **Mars by GHC.** Retrieved May 1, 2023
https://ghc.health/blogs/all-about-men/banana-milk-benefits-a-magical-combination-for-your-Health

Vitamin D. (2012, September 18). Published by **The Nutrition Source.**
Retrieved May 1, 2023 https://www.hsph.harvard.edu/nutritionsource/vitamin-d/

Sunlight and Your Health. (2022, February 22). Published by **WebMD.**
 Retrieved May 1, 2023 https://www.webmd.com/a-to-z-guides/ss/slideshow-sunlight-health-effects

Avoid weight gain this holiday season. (2016, November 26). Published by **The Arab American News**, 32(1607), 20.

Exercise: 7 benefits of regular physical activity. (2021, October 8). Published by **Mayo Clinic.** Retrieved May 1, 2023 https://www.mayoclinic.org/healthy-lifestyle/fitness/in- depth/exercise/art-20048389

Bodybuilding Meal Plan: What to Eat, What to Avoid. (n.d.). Published by **Healthline.** Retrieved May 1, 2023
https://www.healthline.com/nutrition/bodybuilding-meal-plan

Why We Overeat While Watching TV. (2019, December 26). Published by **Cleveland Clinic.** Retrieved May 1, 2023,
https://health.clevelandclinic.org/put-down-that-remote-heres-why-we-overeat-in-front-of-the-tv-and-how-to-stop/

"Breakfast for Learning: Why the Morning Meal Matters." (2023, March 3). Published by **HealthyChildren.org. Retrieved May 1, 2023**https://www.healthychildren.org/English/healthy-living/nutrition/Pages/Breakfast-for-Learning.asp

"Why Get Non-GMO Project Verified" - FoodChain ID. (n.d.). Published by **FoodChainID**.Retrieved May 1, 2023 https://www.foodchainid.com/non-gmo/why-get-non-gmo-project-verified/

Kuzma, J. (2018)." Regulating Gene-Edited Crops. Issues in Science and Technology", 35(1), 80. Avulsion Fracture: Treatments, Recovery, and More. (n.d.). Published by: **Healthline** Retrieved May 1, 2023 https://www.healthline.com/health/avulsion-fracture

A. (2022, May 11). "What's the Difference Between a Fracture and a Break?"Published by **I Cary Ortho. Cary Orthopaedics**. Retrieved May 1, 2023 https://www.caryortho.com/difference-between-a-fracture-and-a-break

"What is blood pressure?" (n.d.). Published by **National Health Service Official Site, UK.** Retrieved May 1, 2023 https://www.nhs.uk/common-health-questions/lifestyle/what-is- blood-pressure/

"Power Outage? Here's How Long the Food in Your Refrigerator and Freezer Lasts." (2023, January 6). Published by **Better Homes & Gardens.** Retrieved May 1, 2023 https://www.bhg.com/recipes/how-to/food-storage-safety/heres-how-long-the-food-in-your-refrigerator- lasts-after-the-power-goes-out/

& Living, V. F. (2019, October 4). "Coconut Oil: Cure or Concern?" - Published by **Vegan Food & Living.** Retrieved May 1, 2023 https://www.veganfoodand living.com/vegan-diet/vegan- nutrition/coconut-oiI-cure-or-concern/

"The Ultimate Home Maintenance Checklist for Year-Round Care." (2023, March 9). Published by **Better Homes & Gardens.** Retrieved May 1, 2023 https://www.bhg.com/home- improvement/advice/home-maintenance-checklist/

Juyal, P. (2021, July 16). "What is the Impact of Late Payment on CIBIL Score? A Comprehensive Guide to Money Transfer, Recharges, Bill Payments, and Other Digital Payments" Published by **Paytm Blog.** Retrieved May 1, 2023 https://paytm.com/blog/credit-score/impact-of-late-payment-on-cibil-score/

Made in United States
North Haven, CT
15 December 2023

45788379R00174